CASEBOOK ON CHURCH AND SOCIETY

Edited by Keith R. Bridston, Fred K. Foulkes,
Ann D. Myers, and Louis Weeks

CASE-
BOOK
ON CHURCH AND SOCIETY

CASE-BOOK

ON CHURCH AND SOCIETY

*Edited by Keith R. Bridston, Fred K. Foulkes,
Ann D. Myers, and Louis Weeks*

Nashville   Abingdon Press   New York

CASEBOOK ON CHURCH AND SOCIETY

Copyright © 1974 by Abingdon Press

Main entry under title:
Casebook on church and society.
Bibliography: p.
1. Theology, Practical—Case studies. 2. Church and social
problems—Case studies. I. Bridston, Keith R., ed.
BV3.C37   261.8'3   74-13419

Library of Congress Cataloging in Publication Data

ISBN 0-687-04709-9

Scripture quotations unless otherwise noted are from the
Revised Standard Version of the Bible, copyrighted 1946,
1952, and 1971 by the Division of Christian Education,
National Council of Churches, and are used by permission.

Scripture quotations noted Phillips are from The New Testament in Modern English, copyright 1958 by J. B. Phillips.

MANUFACTURED   BY   THE   PARTHENON   PRESS   IN
NASHVILLE, TENNESSEE, UNITED STATES OF AMERICA

Contents

PART I. The Church: Its Nature and Mission

by Robert Ackerman, Harvard Business School
Division in a church is created when the steeple is
struck by lightning. Issues involve congregational
priorities, leadership roles, interpersonal conflict, and
religious symbolism.

by Gaylord Noyce, Yale Divinity School
A United Church of Christ pastor is trying to decide how to vote in an upcoming meeting of the association. Issues involve ministry, sexuality, church
government, and ordination.

(A) A Presbytery considers action when one of its
number is ordained, yet also becomes confirmed and
licensed as a lay reader in the Episcopal Church. Issues involve church unity, church polity, church
(B) Describes outcome of the situation. Issues

PART II. The Church: Its Ministry

PART III. *The Church: Community Issues*

counseling, Christian priorities, and organizational behavior.

by Louis Weeks
A concerned layman visits a dying person and is asked to advise the family on a course of action. Issues involve death and dying, interpersonal relationships, counseling, and technological impacts on decision-making.

by Donald Miller, Bethany Theological Seminary
A denominational committee works to recommend an official stance for the communion on a controversial issue. Issues involve abortion, human behavior, organizational behavior, church polity, and conflict management.

PART IV. *Methodology of Cases*

by Fred K. Foulkes, Harvard Business School
Rationale for the case method at Harvard Business School examined for possible parallels to theological education. Issues involve social responsibility, power and change, human behavior, organizational behavior, ethics and personal values, and by implication, church priorities.

by Ann D. Myers and Louis Weeks

Introduction

Nothing is more fatal to the artist than straining to find new subjects. . . . Any aspect of reality, when meditated on and explored to its depths becomes a universe.

—Ignazio Silone

The Case-Study Institute, funded by a grant from the Sealantic Fund, Inc. and sponsored by the American Association of Theological Schools in cooperation with the Boston Theological Institute and more recently with the Graduate Theological Union, was set up to explore the use of the case method in theological education. Using the Harvard Business School, which has long pioneered in case-oriented teaching, as the initial curricular and pedagogical model the program of the institute has focused on introducing teachers of theology to the method, and training them through an annual summer workshop in the writing and teaching of cases.

The main source of the cases in this book are the graduates of the summer workshop held in Cambridge at the Boston Theological Institute and the Harvard Business School. The cases represent issues involving the internal life of the church, the ministry, and the relations between religious organizations and society. In a microcosmic manner they suggest the infinite variety and complexity of the life and mission of church and its ministry in today's world.

Primarily designed as classroom instruments for facilitating reflection on and discussion of critical issues facing the churches today, these cases are by no means relevant only to students of theology planning to become professional clergy. They might well be studied and discussed by practicing ministers and lay persons as part of their continuing theological education, and it is hoped that this volume will be used in that wider circle of concerned church people.

When I wrote *Theological Training in the Modern World* (Geneva, 1954), an international survey of seminary education sponsored by the World's Student Christian Federation and the World Council of Churches, one of the persistent problems identified by both students and faculty was the schism between the theoretical and practical disciplines. One of the values of the case study method is that it brings theory and practice into conjunction. An article in *Fortune* (February, 1972) on the Harvard Business School says of their case discussions: "Perhaps the most helpful, practical thing the students learn is how to construct logical ways to attack almost any conceivable business problem. They are taught to break the problem down, analyze it, and make strategic decisions based on facts." This is "indispensable," says Professor B. J. Matthews, for those "whose careers will depend on their ability to answer questions that have not even been asked yet." It might be argued that most of the great theological questions have already been asked and continue to be pondered. But the forms in which they come change, and the situations which provoke them constantly alter, so that the relation between theory and practice is a perennial one. In any event, by concentrating on concrete, real cases the theological student (in the broadest sense of that term) is literally forced to allow the theories to be corrected by reality and practice to be informed by theory.

There is another important confluence which the case method facilitates, but cannot guarantee. That is the often-separated streams of congregational life and of theological research and academic scholarship. To some extent the "existential questions" (in Paul Tillich's sense) with which academic theology wrestles—or ought to—are most clearly discerned in the everyday life of parishes and in the histories of the men and women in them. Thus, by being the source of the real-life cases studied and discussed by the professional theologians, the congregations help to shape the theological agenda and to determine the priorities within it, just as the problems of the church at Corinth provide the skeletal structure for St. Paul's theological—even metaphysical and mystical—reflections and his prophetic and dogmatic pronouncements.

In this respect at least, the whole theological enterprise might be considered a total system, defined by R. E. Corigan and R. A. Kaufman as, "The sum total of parts making up a whole, including their interactions, which operate within defined performance limits and design constraints while achieving stated mission objectives for the total system." (*Why System Engineering* [Belmont, 1965]) Through the means of cases, parish life is acknowledged as an integral part of the theological system and a part of the whole which enables that system to be open and therefore with the potentiality of continuing life: "Open systems import some form of energy from the external environment. The cell receives oxygen from the air and food from the external world. . . . Similarly, social organizations must also draw renewed supplies of energy from other institutions, or people, or the material environment. No social structure is self-sufficient or self-contained." (D. Katz and R. L. Kahn, "Properties of Open Systems" in F. E. Emery, ed., *Systems Thinking* [London, 1969]) The same might be said to apply, I believe, to intellectual systems like theology.

But the excitement of theology lies in doing it and not simply talking about it. Hopefully this book will engage a wider group in that task than has hitherto been true. For theological teachers and students it may provide a textbook for particular courses, or an integrative means of encouraging interdisciplinary dialogue. For practicing clergy it may be useful for discussion purposes in their professional associations. For laity it may offer a medium for theological group study and discussion relatively free of technical jargon and abstract terminology. For all, it is hoped that it may be a contribution to the clarification of the purposes of religious communities and institutions in our day and the role they and their members may play in the building up of the whole human fellowship in our time.

It should be pointed out, finally, that the cases developed in this book were prepared as bases for class discussion rather than as illustrations of either effective or ineffective handling of administrative situations. Names and places in the case studies are disguised with the exception of those in part 1, chapters 2, 3 and 4.

Keith R. Bridston

CASE-
BOOK
ON CHURCH AND
SOCIETY

CASE-
BOOK
ON CHURCH AND
SOCIETY

PART I
The Church:
Its Nature and Mission

Chapter 1
Walnut Avenue Church

prepared by Robert Ackerman

Harry Tillotson, moderator of the Walnut Avenue Church, was uncertain about what he should do next to help resolve a problem that had deeply divided his congregation. The difficulty, which began when lightning severely damaged the church's historic steeple in September, had, by the following January, come to involve in Mr. Tillotson's mind some fundamental questions concerning how and for what purpose the church was to govern its affairs. The following several pages include, first, a description of Walnut Avenue Church and, second, a summary of the events surrounding the steeple episode.

Walnut Avenue Church

Walnut Avenue Church was Congregational in polity and tradition and located in the downtown section of a middle-sized industrial city on the outskirts of Philadelphia. The church, dating back to colonial times, had a membership of nine hundred of whom approximately four hundred were active members. As is typical of most churches in this sociological situation, its membership had gradually been declining over the past several decades as people moved to surrounding suburban areas. Walnut Avenue Church had remained, however, feeling it had a ministry to the city and its people and was highly regarded in church and lay circles as a responsible and dedicated institution.

The congregation was highly diverse in age and interests. About half the church family were older people, many having children who had grown and left the city. There were only a few families in the thirty to fifty age bracket with growing children. Slightly less than half the congregation were younger people, both single and married, in college and working, many of them related to the universities located nearby. The youth education program was modest in size.

Between annual meetings, the church was governed by the prudential committee, composed of the chairpersons of standing committees, the entire board of deacons, the treasurer, secretary, two members elected at large, and the moderator, who acted as chairperson. Members of all committees, including designated chairpersons, were placed for election by the nominating committee before the congregation at the annual meeting. The elections were not contested, and there had rarely been a dissenting vote. Mr. Tillotson, in six years as moderator, had confined his role to assembling agenda and chairing meetings of the congregation and prudential committee.

The prudential committee approved the budget before it was submitted to the congregation for final ratification. In recent years the church had had to strain to maintain its level of activities though it was fortunate to have a small endowment to ease the impact of fluctuations in pledging. The fund-raising and investment management functions were handled by the finance and property committee, which also had responsibility for the church building. Over time this committee had come to view itself as responsible for the "secular affairs" of the church—those matters involving money and physical assets.

During the past several years, the mission and community committee had expanded its activities beyond making contributions to traditional charitable and denominational agencies and participated in social action programs of various kinds, sometimes involving modest expenditures of funds. On one occasion the committee asked for and received approval from a special meeting of the congregation for a resolution expressing

support and concern for the black community during disturbances in a nearby ghetto area. The resolution was sent to the
mayor and referred to in the press. The committee, and especially its chairperson, had subsequently drawn strong criticism
from some in the parish who felt the use of the resolution to be
"quasi-political" and hence, inappropriate.

The Church Steeple

On a Friday night in September lightning struck the steeple
igniting a fire which caused severe structural damage.

The following morning the finance and property committee
met in emergency session. They concluded that an architect
should be engaged immediately to ascertain the extent of the
damage and the probable cost of repairs. Three days later the
architect reported that emergency measures were necessary to
ensure that the steeple would not collapse on the next windy
day. He also informed the committee that these measures, cost-
ing about a thousand dollars, were not sufficient, and that
either the steeple should be taken down or completely rebuilt at
a cost he thought would run about forty thousand dollars. After
some discussion, the committee told the architect to proceed
with the emergency work and that Fred Thornton, chairman of
the committee, would contact him about further steps to be
taken. After the architect left, the committee, without dissent,
agreed that the steeple ought to be rebuilt and a special gift
campaign should be organized to raise money to cover the cost.

At a special meeting of the prudential committee the following week, Fred Thornton traced what had happened and presented a recommendation to rebuild the steeple. The response
was immediate.

"In a time like this, with all the poverty and problems in the
city, and world refugees and war and all, how can we justify
this much money on a steeple which has no function, even for
us?" asked Danny Cranston, chairman of the mission and
community committee.

"Because," replied Fred Thornton, "if we don't fix it, it will
fall down, and if we take it down, who will know this is a
church?"

An elderly gentleman, Richard Gilroy, a loyal churchman and substantial giver, then offered to contribute a neon-lighted cross, to go atop the repaired steeple so that the whole neighborhood would see the church identified by this radiant symbol.

Though there were no immediate remarks expressing negative feelings about the cross, several scowls from members implied to Mr. Tillotson a twofold problem. How could one stand out against the cross without hurting Mr. Gilroy, and if his gift were refused, would it jeopardize his sizable pledge, which was almost 10 percent of the entire budget? However, Henrietta Gibson, a deacon, came to his support, saying, "This church is the church of my childhood, and I want the steeple to stay on. I know there are many others who feel the same way about it. The finance and property committee voted unanimously to fix the steeple, and if Mr. Gilroy wants to put a cross up there, we ought to go along."

Carlotta Carlyle, another deacon, who said she had joined the church because she thought it could work to bring changes in society, was aghast at this and literally shouted to the meeting, "The world is going to pot, and we sit here discussing spending money on a steeple. It seems to me we have our priorities turned upside down. Jesus sent the church out to minister to mankind, not to make monuments out of our buildings."

The moderator, by now ill at ease, suggested a subsequent meeting because it was now already 11:00 P.M. Mr. Thornton indicated that he felt his committee ought to secure a detailed estimate of the cost of rebuilding. Wallace Berry, chairperson of the music and arts committee, then said that since the bells were a part of the music program, his committee ought to be represented. After some discussion, this latter suggestion was put aside on the ground that the matter could best be handled by finance and property at this stage. Mr. Berry was encouraged, however, to secure the views of his committee before the next prudential committee meeting.

During the ensuing month, the Reverend John Anderson, who had kept his opinions on the matter to himself, preached on the virtues of compassion, forgiveness, acceptance, and brotherly love and reconciliation. He also began to visit Tillotson and Thornton to try to reach an accommodation that would not split the church. Mr. Thornton had urged him to pave the way for conciliation in his preaching. He had also been heard to say, "These ministers don't know anything about money and bricks and real estate values; they ought to stick to spiritual matters." He further implied that as a friend of Richard Gilroy, he thought that if the steeple didn't get fixed and the cross were refused, Gilroy might very well withdraw his membership and pledge.

By the end of October, when a second meeting of the prudential committee was called, the finance and property committee had secured estimates from three builders and after much consultation settled on one for $50,000. Although the estimates were roughly comparable in price (the others were $46,400 and $53,000), the choice was complicated by the great many factors to be considered—design, finish, etc. The recommendation, including the neon cross at an additional cost of $3,500, was put in a motion to the prudential committee.

In the following debate, Wallace Berry noted that while his committee (in a three-to-two vote, with two members absent) was in favor of retaining the steeple and the bells, he personally opposed it and was uncertain how to vote on the motion. One deacon responded by saying, "I think this whole thing is getting out of hand. Let's let those who want to have the steeple replaced raise the money among themselves and leave the rest of us out of it."

Another member answered, "But that is no way for a Christian community to behave—we must learn to work and worship together!"

Eventually the motion was brought to a vote. It lost eleven to nine with Mr. Anderson abstaining. A resolution was then passed respectfully declining Mr. Gilroy's gift but thanking him for his generosity and thoughtfulness.

Through Christmas the atmosphere was tense. The finance and property committee refused to do anything at all in the way of arranging for the removal of the steeple. The Reverend Mr. Anderson, bearing the brunt of well-intentioned but often harsh criticism from some parishioners, began to feel isolated and alone.

Finally, in mid-January, Mr. Tillotson was informed that a meeting of the congregation was being called by a group of parishioners, including several on the finance and property committee, to consider a motion having the effect of reversing the prudential committee vote. Should this motion carry, a second one was to be made requesting that the moderator appoint a committee on governance to consider changes in the bylaws that would have the effect of involving the congregation more directly in the decision-making process in the church.

It was in this situation that Mr. Tillotson pondered over the nature of the church's purpose and what, if anything, he could do to help resolve Walnut Avenue Church's current dilemma.

Preparation Questions

1. How well do you think the steeple incident has been handled?

2. What should the congregation do about the steeple?

3. What responsibilities does the prudential committee have in resolving the problem?

4. What responsibility do individual committees have in resolving it?

5. How should Wallace Berry have voted?

6. Was the finance and property committee justified in not acting to have the steeple removed after the December prudential committee meeting?

7. Should the organization structure be changed by amending the bylaws? How, in broad terms?

8. What should Harry Tillotson do at the end of the case?

Chapter 2
Ecclesiastical Council
prepared by Gaylord Noyce

"Never before has any major religious group knowingly ordained a homosexual—Bill Johnson has a lot to offer us. I hate to slap him down—Am I right to hold on to my enormous resistance to this whole idea?"

These were a few of the thoughts racing through the mind of Jerry Conwell, heterosexual, happily married minister of a five hundred-member congregation of the United Church of Christ near San Francisco. He was now sitting in the crowded, tense Ecclesiastical Council of the Golden Gate Association, United Church of Christ, April 30, 1972. "How the hell am I going to vote?" he asked himself.

Bill Johnson, the candidate, had wanted to be a minister since he was seventeen—five years after he discovered that he was homosexual. He and his two brothers had been active in First Evangelical Church, Houston, Texas, and he was president of both his local youth fellowship and the Houston Christian Youth Council.

From Houston he went to Elmhurst College, Illinois. There, although his sexual orientation was no secret, he became a leader in student government, an active participant in a service fraternity, and presently a member of Omicron Delta Kappa,

This material was prepared by Professor Noyce as the basis for class discussion rather than an illustration of either effective or ineffective handling of an administrative situation. It is primarily an adaptation of reports by W. Evan Golder in *United Church Herald* and *Christian Century*.

the leadership honorary fraternity. Following college he entered Pacific School of Religion at Berkeley, "convinced that God had called (him) to the ordained ministry."

Jerry looked again at Bill as he thought about his vote. Johnson was twenty-six, a moderately tall, gentle-mannered person, with resolute blue-gray eyes that looked tougher than the soft roundness of his face. Jerry felt that Bill's answers in the general examination had been direct and to the point, his ordination paper a good one. Here was a man who seemed to know what he was about—more so, confessed Jerry to himself, than he had when he was ordained twenty-five years earlier.

While he was still in seminary, Bill Johnson decided he would be "up front" with the church about his sexual identity. At a seminary symposium on homosexuality in November, 1970, he "came out of his closet" and affirmed that he was "gay." He explained in his ordination paper: "Persons whom I respect counseled against such honesty. It would have been much easier—much more expedient—to remain silent. But I do not believe the call to discipleship is a call to expediency. I could not personally, in good conscience, take the vows of ordination without fully affirming who I am."

Later in the paper, Johnson said he was aware that his openness about his sexuality risked his being denied ordination. But his sense of call was so strong he felt he had no choice. "I am compelled by the power of the Holy Spirit at work in my life," he wrote. "It is no longer I who have chosen the ordained ministry as a profession. I have been chosen." Jerry Conwell was not so sure.

In United Church of Christ polity, a request for ordination must originate with a local congregation. The Board of Deacons of the San Carlos Community Church, where Bill had worked as a student assistant, made such a request of the Church and Ministry Committee of the Northern California Conference. This committee interviewed him twice, found his credentials in order, and pronounced him "well qualified in all aspects of training, theology, experience." But it voted, in May, 1971, by a split vote of four to three *not* to recommend him for ordination. In the United Church of Christ the right to ordain, however, rests with the local association, not with the conference-level hierarchy. Thus, the final decision had to be made by the Golden Gate Association of thirty-one local congregations. Bill Johnson had proceeded to request of that association a decision on ordination. Recognizing the profound questions involved and the emotional tensions gathering around the request, the association leadership asked for time and set up a task force to educate clergy and lay delegates of the association on the issues. The task force organized two all-day sessions on homosexuality and ordination and arranged several evening dialogues between Bill and small church groups.

Beyond training and a sense of personal vocation, United Church of Christ polity also expects a candidate for ordination to have a "call" to ministry in some particular place of service. After his 1971 completion of seminary, Bill Johnson had moved to Hollywood, where he got a job as a bank teller. His evenings and weekends he spent working with the United Church of Christ Tentmaker Ministry, a successful new program in the Los Angeles area for reaching people who are disillusioned with the church. Thus, Bill Johnson's call came from this denominationally supported Tentmaker project.

About once a month Bill commuted north for meetings arranged by the Golden Gate Association's committee. Jerry Conwell had attended one of these meetings—in Tiburon, in February. It had been a tense meeting. Association moderator Bonnie Ploeger warned the sixty-five middle-class whites attending that they were in a national fishbowl. "The vote to take place in April will have its impact in churches all across the country," she stressed, "not just in this association or this denomination, but in all churches."

Panelists at the meeting had included a psychiatrist, a seminary professor, a parish minister, and a "gay" attorney. The meeting seemed to Jerry to be loaded in favor of ordaining Johnson, even though the task force chairman, pastor of the Mill Valley Church said, "We did not invite you here to try to make up your minds for you.

The psychiatrist said that people in his field are divided over the causes of homosexuality. It is a "wide-open question." And he added, "So is what causes heterosexuality, since all other species of mammals practice both homosexual and heterosexual behavior. We need to re-examine our categories and our understanding in the light of new data."

The parish minister rebutted the argument by saying that some psychiatrists see homosexuality to be the result of arrested emotional development. "If there ever was a time in the church when we needed emotionally competent leadership, it is now, and on that basis I would oppose this proposed ordination."

The seminary professor denounced the idea that homosexuality in itself is sinful. "Sin, or wrongness," he explained, "is not characterized by any single sexual style. The most crucial factor is the quality of the personal relationship. If a person uses sex as an opportunity to exploit another, that is sinful."

The ensuing discussion soon became heated, and Jerry noticed how Bill Johnson, sitting quietly in the back of the room, had bent lower, staring at the tiled floor. Many who were present did not know he was present. One retired minister was certain that Johnson's homosexuality was simply a state of mind which he could change if he wished. "The church is not here to accept people as they are," he insisted. "The church asks people to change, and I changed, and I've seen homosexuals change." A woman on the other side of the room responded promptly, "Something really bothers me there; I always thought Jesus accepted people as they were."

Other questions flew back and forth that night. "Can homosexuals be cured?" "Would the church be in the position of hiring a known lawbreaker?" "If we ordain this man, won't it attract more homosexuals to the church?" "How will we present this to our congregations?" The last question troubled Jerry Conwell especially, every time he thought that the association might proceed with the ordination. His congregation had already found this issue the chief subject matter in any discussion of denominational affairs; the church was split right down the middle on the issue.

Jerry also thought over the competence of Bill Johnson, however. "Bill has a great sensitivity toward people," someone had declared at the task force meeting. "He'll make an exceptional minister."

A young man stood up, hands firmly on his hips. "Homosexual is a label, like nigger or Jew. We overreact. I've known Bill ever since I was a high school sophomore, and now I'm a sophomore in college. There's nothing wrong with Bill. He's just as healthy as you or I."

"I don't know a more qualified young man seeking to go into the ministry," said one woman, the mother of teen-agers in the youth group Bill had served while in seminary.

But another delegate opposed her: "This thing will tear the churches apart. We should not put our stamp of approval upon homosexuality."

Conwell had left that meeting still undecided. His parish work kept him too busy to work thoroughly at the issue, but he found here and there some reports of other church pronouncements. His own denomination's Council for Christian Social Action had called in 1969 for repeal of all laws against private homosexual relations between consenting adults, and had urged member churches to hold "honest and open discussion of the nature of homosexuality in our society." The denomination's Council on Church and Ministry had not taken any position when it discussed the pending Golden Gate Association decision.

The 182nd General Assembly of the United Presbyterian Church in the U.S.A. had reaffirmed "that adultery, prostitution, fornication and/or the practice of homosexuality is sin," but it did call on churches "to support and give leadership in movements toward the elimination of laws governing the private sexual behavior of consenting adults."

A similar statement was approved by the American Lutheran Church's Commission on Research and Social Action in 1970. It declared that "homosexual behavior is contrary to God's creation," but also insisted that "the church should not demand that criminal law restrict the private behavior of mutually consenting adults."

Jerry was also aware that the original Northern California Conference Church and Ministry Committee, the one which had rejected Bill Johnson's request for ordination in the spring of 1971, had unanimously *adopted* the following more positive statement in November:

If a candidate for ordination chooses openly to declare his or her sexual identity to be homosexual, this should not in itself be considered a disqualification for ordination, but rather this should be seen in the light of the candidate's total view of human sexuality and understanding of the morality of its use.

Pressures on Jerry's vote had been mounting steadily. Along with all other members of the ecclesiastical council, he had received a letter from the Reverend James Clark Borwn, pastor of the prestigious First Congregational Church of San Francisco: "I prayerfully petition you to consider the untapped and enormous potential for Christ-like ministry which resides within many homosexually oriented persons. It is tragic that both they and the church have so long been denied the use of their gifts."

On April 30, in the afternoon, it was like Easter Sunday at San Carlos Community Church. Visitors were lined up waiting to get in. Inside, the church was full, with the voting delegates sitting in the front pews—fifty-six lay persons and forty clergy. All United Church of Christ ministers "with standing," living in the association, were entitled to vote, whether or not currently working in a local church. In addition, each congregation was allotted a certain number of lay voting delegates, depending on its size. Nineteen churches sent delegations.

Scheduled to begin at 3:30, the council finally opened twenty-five minutes late. Following an opening prayer and a hymn, the state conference's credentials committee report was received—*not* recommending ordination although Johnson's credentials were in order. Then Bill Johnson stood up and started to read his ordination paper. He read with calmness and conviction. There was hushed silence as he traced his religious development from his youth to the present. He mentioned his homosexuality briefly, affirming, "I value honesty and integrity." It was only toward the end of his paper, as he moved into theology, that the congregation began to cough and shift about. He finished, and a five-minute break was announced.

Then the open examination of the candidate began. The first question was direct. "Do you regard homosexuality as a gift from God and a good gift?"

Johnson's answer was equally direct. "I regard *all* sexuality as a gift from God and a good gift."

A second question was raised. "As a homosexual minister, how would you relate to prostitutes?"

Johnson answered, "I believe that the style of Christ himself gives us that answer."

The conference minister asked: "What type of ministry do you have in mind?"

Johnson replied: "I remain open to God's guidance. Anyone who knows me knows that I'm deeply committed to the parish church."

At that point someone else interjected: "'Wouldn't you be a negative example to young people?"

Pointing to the young people in the balcony who had joined the church when he had been an assistant there Johnson replied, "I always try to relate to other human beings as I would expect to be related to, not exploiting another human being, not manipulating anyone."

"Would you be willing to forego the personal pleasures of homosexuality in order to accept ordination?" The crowd gasped audibly.

Johnson hesitated. "I hear you asking the question of celibacy. Is this it?"

"It could be, if the hearer wants to interpret it that way."

He paused again and then said firmly: "I am asking this council to recognize and give its blessing upon my call to the ministry, not to affirm homosexuality. My personal conviction is that I cannot do other than I have done, to be fully honest, and to approach the altar with integrity."

Some letters were introduced. One from Johnson's college president stated: "William Johnson would make a significant contribution to the life of the church." In another letter Bill's own mother said, "It hasn't been easy to accept the fact that I have a son who is a homosexual. But I'd rather have him honest and happy than live a lie and be miserable. He has a hard time pretending to be something he isn't. Ask yourselves, if William hadn't admitted his homosexuality, wouldn't you have ordained him already? I am proud of my son."

More questions followed and tension rose. What did Johnson think about marriage? "I think love between any two people is beautiful and should be celebrated. I know that two men or two women can share such a love."

"What should we expect if we ordain a homosexual?" This question was asked with anger.

"I hope you would expect from me the same responsible style of living that you would expect from any person who is ordained to the ministry."

Questions seemed at an end and the moderator announced, "Coffee is ready for the nonvoting delegates and visitors." The moment for final discussion and a vote had arrived, and Jerry Conwell was even yet not ready for a decision.

Chapter 3
A Delicate
and Difficult Matter

A

The Presbytery of Hanover had a difficult decision to make. On Ascension Day, May 15, 1969, one of its ministers, the Reverend J. A. Ross Mackenzie, who was a professor of church history at Union Theological Seminary in Richmond, Virginia, was confirmed by the Bishop of Virginia in St. Peter's Church. Present at the simple ceremony were the vicar of the church, two vestrymen of the predominantly black congregation, the president of the seminary, and Flora Mackenzie, the professor's wife.

With his certificate of confirmation Dr. Mackenzie also received a lay reader's license to administer the chalice during the Communion at St. Peter's. The question of confirmation had been earlier discussed at length by the bishop and the professor. "I wanted to be absolutely legal in what I was doing," Mackenzie reflected later, "and I wanted to take part in serving during the Communion. This was to be possible as a licensed lay reader." The action, however, aroused considerable controversy within the denomination, and was eventually appealed to the General Assembly itself for a decision.

Asked to pass a judgment on the legality of the act, Ben L. Rose, a colleague at Union Seminary and an authority on the Presbyterian *Book of Church Order*, expressed his mind: "Joining another denomination *is* tantamount to renouncing the

This case was prepared as a basis for class discussion rather than an illustration of either effective or ineffective handling of a situation. Copyright © 1973 The Case-Study Institute.

authority or communion of our Church. In his own mind, Dr. Mackenzie has not renounced the authority of the Presbyterian Church, but according to the *Book of Church Order,* he has! The only action that I see that Hanover Presbytery can take is to require Dr. Mackenzie to relinquish his membership in the Episcopal Church, and if he refuses, then withdraw his authority to exercise his office in the Presbyterian Church." The letter concluded, "A great deal is at stake" (Exhibit 1).

Ross Mackenzie was born in Scotland in 1927, and after receiving his degrees from the University of Edinburgh was ordained to the ministry of the Church of Scotland.

"I was trained for the ministry in St. Giles' Cathedral," he said in explanation of his liturgical interests. "At St. Giles we celebrated the Holy Communion every Sunday. I've never forgotten the thrill I felt whenever the bread and wine were carried solemnly into the church by the elders, while the congregation sang the psalm, 'Ye gates lift up your heads on high.' Later I went to a new church on the outskirts of the city in a low-cost housing development, and we continued the practice of weekly Communion there. With a great deal of opposition, let it be said! But I thought it should be done. After all, Calvin in Geneva had wanted a weekly celebration of the Lord's Supper, and I tried to show people that this was very much part of our Reformed tradition.

"One of the people who influenced me very strongly in those days was a priest of the Episcopal Church in Scotland. He'd inherited a run-down Anglo-Catholic parish, and was extremely interested in the kind of liturgical renewal that was very much involved in social and political concerns. You know, the Parish and People program, the Frontier Group, and all that. We used to meet every month in his rectory; management and labor people, trade unionists, teachers, and some of us church folk. The liturgy in his church on Sunday expressed all this. He'd pulled the altar out into the center, made the service much more of a people's service. His church always had the fragrance of incense about it . . . as well as posters of skinny children in Africa or India.

"It was this double interest—worship and social concerns —that led me to join the Iona Community. George MacLeod, the leader of the community, was one of the greatest influences on my life, I think. A remarkable man. Pacifist, socialist, high churchman. You have to experience the worship in Iona Abbey to know what it means to be haunted by the *mysterium tremendum*. But my interest wasn't just in liturgical millinery. I got involved in the local Labor Party in my parish, and got into plenty of trouble because of that.

"For these and other reasons I've also had a strong involvement in church unity and ecumenical questions. I'd studied in Lutheran Sweden. I'd taught at Catholic University. I was one of the delegates of the Presbyterian Church, U.S., in the Consultation on Church Union. And I'd served as one of the Reformed representatives in the bilateral consultations with the Roman Catholic Church. I'd like to try to build bridges between the denominations. Right now, church union is a far-off goal, but it's still possible to bridge the separations and find a common means of working together. Let me just quote from a thing I wrote in 1966."

Mackenzie reached across to a filing cabinet and pulled out a page.

"It says, 'To be true to the Reformers does not mean petrifying the form of the church and the formulation of its faith into unalterable structures. That way lies the idolatry of the church. To be truly "Reformed" does mean that by listening afresh to the Word of God as a reality higher than our own traditions, as that which judges us and our past, and calls us into a new future, we are drawn into a truly new and lively community —something which is not our making, but God's.' "

The events of Ascension Day, 1969, were published in the August issue of the Episcopalian *Virginia Churchman* under the headline, "Confirmation Gives New Role to Presbyterian Clergyman." The report spoke of his loyalty both to the Presbyterian Church, in which he cherished his authority to preach and to celebrate Holy Communion, and to the Episcopalian Church, in which he had discovered the richness of corporate worship, the opportunity to serve outside the affluent white culture in which he was usually thrown, and the possibility of the reality of Christianity over against denominationalism. The report ended:

"There is no question raised about the validity of my Presbyterian orders," Dr. Mackenzie said, "I remain loyal to the Presbyterian Church. At the same time, I want to discover ways to break down the walls of separation and bridge the gaps for genuine reconciliation. Our wounds need to be healed."

The report of the confirmation was printed in the August 25 issue of an independent and generally liberal periodical, *Presbyterian Outlook*. Noting that neither Bishop Gibson nor Dr. Mackenzie could be reached to discuss the implications of the action, the report stressed that the original proposal had not had the approval of Hanover Presbytery, and had not even been discussed by that body prior to the act of confirmation. A section of the *Book of Church Order* was then cited, the interpretation of which was to become a crucial part of the subsequent debate:

When a church officer, whether minister, ruling elder, or deacon, renounces the communion or authority of this church by a statement or by joining some other church recognized by our own as a true branch of the Church of Christ, the court having jurisdiction shall record the irregularity and withdraw from him all authority to exercise office derived from this church. . . .

A church officer who has renounced the jurisdiction of this church and who desires to be restored shall apply to the same church court under whose jurisdiction he was when his relationship with this communion was severed. The court shall hear him, and, if satisfied, may restore his membership. In the case of a former minister, the presbytery shall assign him to membership in some particular church subject to the approval of the session of that church. Restoration to office in the church can be accomplished only by passing through all the steps necessary for a man's being called to office in the church for the first time, including ordination" (*Book of Church Order*, 111:3-4, "Procedural Rules for Informal Disposition [Cases Without Process]: Renouncing the Jurisdiction of the Church").

The confirmation and the two reports of it in the *Virginia Churchman* and *Presbyterian Outlook* were reported briefly in a Richmond daily newspaper. Two short comments were added.

Dr. Mackenzie was reported to have said that his confirmation was "a purely personal matter of where I exercise my Christian discipleship." A spokesman for the Episcopal Diocese of Virginia said that baptism rather than confirmation constituted membership in the church.

The editor of the *Presbyterian Outlook*, Dr. Aubrey N. Brown, Jr., discussed the matter fully in an editorial September 8.

On the side of the minister, serious questions of procedure must be faced in relation to his obligation to the presbytery and the presbytery's obligation to the church-at-large. It is understood that a minister is governed by his presbytery in these relationships. That such a significant step should have been taken without conference with and approval by the presbytery is highly irregular. If such relationships are to be entered upon at the will of the minister, then what part does he feel that presbytery plays in his ministry after all?

If there are irregularities on the Presbyterian side of this transaction, there are even more serious ones on the Episcopal side, for it is little short of astonishing that anyone so obviously committed to deepening the good relationships between the churches as demonstrated in his leadership in the Consultation on Church Union, should, as the Bishop of Virginia seems to have done, have entered into a unilateral relationship of the deepest significance to ministry without so much as a by-your-leave to Hanover Presbytery within whose bounds he resides. Had he no concern for what his action would imply about Presbyterian ordination or a minister's sworn obligation to his presbytery? Was he insensitive to the implication that a minister in full standing in the Presbyterian family, a professor in a theological seminary, would not be recognized as such in another Christian church, but rather in an Episcopal church would be given status as a lay reader with permission to prepare his own sermons—and this only upon condition that a bishop's hands were laid upon him in confirmation even though he had been ordained by the laying on of the hands of his presbytery? It is difficult to imagine that Episcopal confirmation customarily has so little regard for the existing relationships of those who are to be confirmed as appears to have been indicated in this instance.

Dr. Mackenzie reflected somewhat later on the mounting concern about the case. "It seems curious to me," he said, "how rigidly defined Aubrey Brown's interpretation is of what is permissible to someone who wants to put good will to work. I get the impression of a very narrow tolerance, as if to say, 'This is all right for you, to minister in this church, but you can't do it, as a minister, in an Episcopal church. Or at least, not in the way you are doing it.' How does this harmonize with the liberalism of the *Outlook?* Aubrey Brown has uncovered an illiberal and unkind vein in his makeup. It was he who sent in an *Outlook* envelope a marked copy of the *Outlook* report to the chairman of Presbytery's Commission. I couldn't help noticing a quotation on the front of the *Outlook* this week: 'Whatever be the dangers of this enterprise, are we permitted to abandon it?' The confirmation at St. Peter's is small enough in itself, but in what it represents it's important."

The response to Mackenzie's action amongst his colleagues and fellow-ministers was mixed. Two were typical. One wrote with a word of commendation: "Frankly, I rejoice in this step of faith—more faith and adventuring trust in the providence of God than I have seen to be customary in the Presbyterian Church, U.S. As one who is frustrated by our church's obsession with legalisms and minutiae, I am excited (rather than frightened) by the implications of your action." A blunt interview with a colleague was much more critical. "You have betrayed my church," the colleague said angrily. He was asked what he meant. "I mean that by your action you have said that neither your own confirmation nor your ordination have any validity. Ross, this was a silly, irresponsible act. You have conceded everything to the Episcopalian side. Someone in your position should act with much greater caution. What you have done is to renounce both your ministry and your membership in the Presbyterian Church. And you've fallen back into your usual course of covering your actions in rhetoric."

From that time relations between Mackenzie and his colleague were strained, and an atmosphere was created in which it was impossible to converse. Some of his friends drew up a letter supporting the spirit if not the form of the act, but the proposal to publish it was quietly dropped as inappropriate at that time.

In the meantime Hanover Presbytery had begun to investigate the question through its Commission on the Minister and His Work. The chairman of the commission, the Reverend Glenn Dickson, first sought an explanation from Bishop Gibson. In his letter Bishop Gibson said: "In my intention and in my understanding, Dr. Mackenzie did not renounce his membership or orders in the Presbyterian Church, nor did he become a member of the Episcopal Church. By his confirmation he did satisfy a technical legal requirement which then permitted me to license him to perform certain functions within the Episcopal Church" (Exhibit 2).

Another whose advice on the matter was sought was the scholarly historian, Dr. Ernest Trice Thompson, a former moderator of the church's General Assembly, and generally regarded as a liberal in his outlook. Dr. Thompson addressed himself to the question of the meaning of the *Book of Church Order*, paragraph 111:3-4. "Formally," he said, "it does seem to apply to Dr. Mackenzie's case. It seems to suggest that an officer renounces the communion or authority of the Presbyterian Church, U.S., by either a declaration to this effect, or simply by becoming a member of some other church—as I judge Dr. Mackenzie has done in his act of confirmation. I doubt, however, whether the General Assembly and the presbyteries in voting this provision had any such situation in mind. There was no discussion at the time that I am aware of that would throw light on this question, but I presume what the fathers had in mind was the possible case where an officer would as it were walk out of the Presbyterian Church by going off into another denomination." Dr. Thompson ended the letter by suggesting a way of approaching the General Assembly for its advice on whether a minister might also be a confirmed member of an Episcopal or some other church (Exhibit 3).

The vicar of St. Peter's (the Reverend Edward Meeks Gregory) wrote to the Bishop Coadjutor (the Right Reverend Robert B. Hall) with an interpretation that differed from that of Bishop Gibson: "My memory and records indicate that, having been baptized in the Church of Scotland and having expressed his desire to become a member of the Episcopal Church, John Anderson Ross Mackenzie was so enrolled—it being perfectly clear that he was a loyal Presbyterian minister who had no intention of dropping or compromising his Presbyterian connection. He understood this. I understood this. We both spoke to the Bishop about it and believed he understood this." Father

Gregory's letter raised the question of whether the Presbyterian professor would be forced to choose between his Presbyterian ministry and his membership in the Episcopal Church: "He tells me that he is willing for the issue to be just there, if his challengers should be successful, much as he would regret it. The question which remains to be settled is whether or no the Presbyterians will permit him to remain a minister (or, perhaps, a member) so long as he is an Episcopalian. In short, the present question hangs on whether Ross is or is not *also* an Episcopalian."

Dr. Mackenzie was summoned to meet the Commission on the Minister and His Work on September 30. Four major groups of questions had to be asked:

1. Was he actually a member of the Episcopal Church? What is the meaning of confirmation? What vows did he take? Was he subject to the discipline and authority of the Episcopal Church? What are the responsibilities of a lay reader?

2. Had he renounced his Presbyterian membership and ordination vows?

3. Was the step he had taken in violation of the *Book of Church Order?* Must the commission not do all in its power to protect the integrity of the *Book of Church Order?* Was there a precedent in Presbyterian history for such an action?

4. Why did not Dr. Mackenzie consult with either the commission or presbytery's council and gain presbytery approval before taking the steps he took?

The executive secretary of the presbytery (the Reverend A. M. Hart) and the chairman of the commission had prepared a joint report to be presented at the commission meeting. The report expressed the hope that, though it was regrettable that Dr. Mackenzie had not consulted the presbytery, presbytery would allow him to continue as a lay reader in the Episcopal Church. The irony of the situation was commented upon:

We confess to a certain mixture of amusement and resentment at the rigidity of Episcopal Canon Law, because it requires such a procedure for a brother minister merely to assist in administering the Lord's

Supper and to be able to preach in an Episcopal Church. We are keenly aware of the irony of granting permission "to preach sermons of his own composition" to an eminent professor in one of the leading theological seminaries of the nation, a man who for five years preached in one of the prominent pulpits in the city of Richmond and is a recognized leader in the ecumenical movement. We are sadly cognizant of these canon law requirements, for they imply that Presbyterian ordination is not valid as far as the Episcopal Church is concerned. However, we are sympathetic to Bishop Gibson's responsibility to canon law and conscious that the course he took was the only way in his power to make it possible for Dr. Mackenzie to follow what seemed to him a clear leading of the Holy Spirit."

Finally, the report recommended that the presbytery overture the General Assembly to study barriers to intercommunion in the two denominations.

When the commission met, Dr. Mackenzie and Bishop Hall were both present and both invited to speak. Dr. Mackenzie spoke on his understanding of confirmation. He argued that there was no theological objection to repeating the laying-on of hands. He regarded his confirmation at Bishop Gibson's hands as a "commitment to a new kind of service in addition to the ministry which I exercise joyfully in my own sphere. I do not claim that what I have done is the next step for our church; but I do claim that we shall not know what the next step is or how we may make modifications so as to translate ecumenicity and catholicity into action unless someone takes that step" (Exhibit 4).

Bishop Hall expressed the view that if one accepted the concept of dual membership for the purpose of service within two denominations, it could be held that Dr. Mackenzie was a member of both the Presbyterian Church and the Episcopal Church. This was his own view.

The commission debated at length what its recommendations to the presbytery should be. The report finally agreed upon suggested that Dr. Mackenzie withdraw his name from the parish roll of St. Peter's Church, pending disposition of the matter. The report discussed the varied interpretations of confirmation which were found within the Episcopal Church, and suggested that Bishop Gibson's "theological" interpretation of the rite might be in conflict with the common "ecclesiastical" meaning within the Episcopal Church. It called this a "loophole" through which the bishop had stepped, and then asked: "Is this ambiguity a 'loophole' to be slipped through by well-intentioned individuals to advance the cause of ecumenical good-will, or is it the noose that may strangle our denomination's continuing efforts to express our oneness in Christ?" The commission's report stressed again the regrettable fact that Presbyterian ministers were not recognized by the Episcopal Church:

The Canons of the Episcopal Church which prohibit ordained Presbyterian ministers from administering the sacrament of the Lord's Supper or even assisting an Episcopal priest at the Lord's Table unfortunately make it clear that the validity of the Presbyterian ministry of Word and Sacrament is not recognized. As Bishop Gibson himself admits, "The unhappy result is that *Episcopal laymen* can perform functions which are not legally open to *Presbyterian clergy.*" Although Bishop Gibson apparently deplores this situation, he and we must nevertheless face the fact that the *Canons* of the Episcopal Church and not the *Book of Church Order* of the Presbyterian Church in the United States does not express the ecumenical spirit. We would suggest that if all the branches of the Holy Catholic Church are to be renewed and move toward becoming truly reformed and united, it will not be a movement back into clericalism, but rather a movement forward into the fullness of priesthood of all believers."

The commission concluded its report to the presbytery with certain recommendations: First, that the whole question should be referred to the General Assembly, because it involved "a difficult and delicate matter" affecting both the churches, and also because the meaning of paragraph 111:3 of the *Book of Church Order* was unclear. Second, that the General Assembly also initiate a study on the meaning of confirmation in the Reformed tradition. Third, that the assembly instruct its appropriate committees to study barriers to intercommunion in the polities of the Presbyterian and Episcopal churches.

When the presbytery met at Petersburg on October 28, the commission presented its report for approval. Dr. Mackenzie was invited to speak in explanation of his action. In what a newspaper report the following day called "a moving address"

he outlined for presbytery ten "theses" on the church, speaking
briefly on each of them:

Love is better than hate and reconciliation is better than division, but
we shall never know what love and reconciliation will do until we hear
the Word of God speak to our day.

God is calling into being new patterns of life together, new communities of meaning, and a new era for the church.

We must learn how to take risks in the church.

We shall be unimaginative if we fail to see the extent, the urgency, and
the significance of the revolution of the young.

To be truly Reformed does not mean petrifying the form of the church
and the formulation of its faith into unalterable structures.

What we need is something more radical than Reformation—it is a
renaissance in which we move beyond the reformation of theological
systems and ecclesiastical structures to the transformation of people.

In this whole process the church is pivotal.

Let the church therefore be the church.

We must face our coming Calvary, because the one who has taken the
cross cannot turn back.

We are the pioneers of the new revolution.

The minister said that he did consider himself a member of
both denominations: "I have not renounced my membership or
my ministry in a church to which I have given sixteen years of
service. No ecumenical advance demands that. It does not mean
that in my own ministry or in my work as a teacher in a
seminary of our church I now divide my allegiance or come
under the jurisdiction of any other authority than the one to
which I yield obedience—this presbytery itself." Dr. Mackenzie
argued that the paragraph in the *Book of Church Order* which
implies that such a second denominational membership consti-
tutes renunciation applies to ministers "who deliberately or by
carelessness cut themselves off from fellowship with this
church by attaching themselves to another church which they
prefer."

One of the ministers present wanted the report to be received
as information. "The bishop," he said, "doesn't seem to know

what went on, according to reports. Why could we not allow him (Dr. Mackenzie) to do this?" Another wanted the presbytery to commend him for his pioneering work. Two others rose at once to stress the constitutional issue and the need for a General Assembly judgment. A minister from a north-side Richmond suburb said that commendation by the presbytery would suggest that this would solve the problem which was largely an Episcopal problem. The first minister to speak repeated that receiving as information was the best step, since it would let a man follow his conscience and would permit the Episcopal Church to deal with its problem.

The chairman of the commission, Glenn Dickson, referred to the *Book of Church Order* and its claims. "We have some groups in some parts of the church," he said, "that are not abiding by it." Professor John Newton Thomas supported the commission recommendations as the means of bringing the issue to the assembly. He also proposed deletion of "in the polities" in the commission's report when it requested a study of "the barriers to intercommunion *in the polities* of our church and of the Episcopal Church." Whatever criticisms may be leveled against "our church," he said, "there are in our polity no barriers to intercommunion." Dr. Thomas had been a member of the Faith and Order Movement of the World Council of Churches for many years where the issue of intercommunion had been the subject of prolonged debate. He reviewed the story, pointing out the barriers from the Episcopal side and the failure to make progress in dealing with them. He concluded with the judgment that it was unrealistic to suppose that an assembly's committee could do what the combined churches of the world had failed to do in forty years.

Dr. Mackenzie insisted that "in the polities" should remain, that there were barriers from the Presbyterian side. If not, he asked, what have we been arguing about for an hour and a half?

Dr. Thomas asked Dr. Mackenzie what were the barriers from the Presbyterian side, and the reply was, "Section 111:3, in the opinion of some." The amendment of Dr. Thomas was voted.

A presbytery official sought to commend the spirit of Dr. Mackenzie's action, adding this to the report. Dr. Mackenzie said that this would prejudge the issue, and the addition was not voted.

The minister of a west-end church moved to delete the section in the commission's report asking withdrawal from membership at St. Peter's until the issue was resolved. This was voted, and the report as amended was approved.

Dr. Aubrey Brown, the editor of *Presbyterian Outlook*, was a shy, precise man with graying red hair. He had been critical of the Mackenzie action from the beginning, and in editorials on November 10 and 24, 1969, he wrote:

[There are many people] who are so eager to get on with the job that they become restive at any suggestion of respect for guidelines which have been fashioned out of past centuries of bitter struggle. Sometimes this is born of unimaginative minds which fail to comprehend the ramifications of a problem, sometimes it reflects ignorance of the interplay of historic forces, sometimes it is an act of rebellion at any suggestion of authority.

In the church as in the civil order, provisions for due process have been won at great cost. It would be the height of folly for this guarantee to be tossed overboard in a fit of impatience. The *Book of Church Order* is sometimes difficult to live with, it can be scoffed at as full of legalisms, but its scoffers will someday find that its legalisms bring them the freedom which they enjoy.

This is no plea for meaningless rules and regulations, it is a reminder that some of the regulations which we often scorn in our haste may be part of a system which in a day of urgent need we will seek to recall.

It would be very nice if everyone could do as he liked, but that, after all, is the way to anarchy.

It is good that the Presbyterian, U.S., General Assembly will have the opportunity to deal with the question of how Presbyterians can lend their strength more effectively to the desirable step of extending the ministry of one church so as to include ministry in others.

This is a relatively easy question for Presbyterians. We have long held to and practiced the mutual recognition of ministry. We do not raise bars, we welcome other ministers to join us or to serve as ministers. The reason for this is quite clear. Such ministers were ordained, not into some Presbyterian body, but into the One Holy Catholic Church, and they recognize the same for the ministers of other denominations. Therefore, they do not welcome the implication that their ordination or that of any other was limited, qualified, or insufficient.

With all the criticism of liberalizing trends leveled at Lambeth X, the worldwide decennial gathering of Episcopal bishops, the fact that it displayed a tendency to share freely most of the priestly functions with the laity while not touching the traditional area of difficulty (what to do with the ordained minister upon whom a bishop has not laid his hands) simply underscores the continuing problem.

The request from Hanover Presbytery to the General Assembly for a ruling on the interpretation of paragraph 111:3 of the *Book of Church Order* was received by the assembly's Permanent Judicial Commission at the end of January, 1970. The commission debated the question at length. According to Presbyterian law, the commission was required to make a recommendation to the General Assembly, due to meet at Memphis, Tennessee, late in June of the same year. Procedurally, this recommendation came from the permanent commission to a standing committee of the assembly, where it would be debated before coming to the floor of the assembly for a vote.

All the documents in the case had been presented to the Permanent Judicial Commission, and it made its decision: the General Assembly should decline to hear and make final disposition of the reference. This had the effect of sending the matter back again to the presbytery as the court of primary jurisdiction. However, the permanent commission offered guidance with regard to constitutional interpretation:

1. The Constitution of the Presbyterian Church does not allow dual membership of members or officers, except in specified situations not involved in this matter.
2. "Joining some other church" is of itself renunciation of the communion or authority of this church, and the intention or purpose in joining the other church is not material.
3. The question of whether the member or officer joined another church is to be determined by ordinary and objective standards of the other church, and the intention of the member or officer is not material.
4. The function of Lay Reader in the Episcopal Church involves work not subject to the jurisdiction of Hanover Presbytery, and apart from confirmation and license incident to the office, would require that permission of Presbytery be requested and obtained in advance and a determination be made by Presbytery that the nature of the work is proper to the Ministry of the Gospel, and that the particular work serves the best interest of the church and the minister.

When the executive presbyter of Hanover Presbytery (the Reverend A. M. Hart) read the proposed recommendation, he wondered if a better way might be found out of the dilemma. It appeared to him that the advice which the commission was recommending put the presbytery into an extremely difficult position. "We asked for assistance in a delicate matter," he said, "a matter which is technically difficult but well intentioned in its efforts to bridge an ecumenical chasm." So he prepared a brief regarding the recommendation which he hoped to present to the standing committee before the matter came to a vote on the floor of the assembly:

We feel we are being offered advice which in its implications is punitive to our fellow member and haughty to our brothers in the Episcopal Church who were trying to bridge the chasm within the limitations of their polity.

He suggested that the paragraph in the *Book of Church Order* was not as unequivocal as the commission interpreted it to be. For one thing the heading of the chapter was, "Renouncing the Jurisdiction of the Church." But Dr. Mackenzie had not renounced the jurisdiction of the church. He continued to give his ecclesiastical loyalty and obedience to the presbytery. The paragraph did not state that "joining some other church" is always the equivalent of renouncing the communion and authority of the church. The possibility had never occurred to the framers of the *Book of Church Order* that a person might join a second church without intending to renounce the first. The recommended interpretation appeared to call for Hanover Presbytery to summarily end the career, usefulness, and ministry of a consecrated and able servant of God. Was it really the will of the assembly that the matter be handled in such a tragic and unfeeling way as that?

For these reasons, Mr. Hart went on, the standing committee should explore the possibility of substituting one of the following options for the entire report of the Permanent Judicial Commission on this matter.

1. Request some sort of joint committee of the Presbyterian Church and the Episcopal Church to explore this matter in

the light of the polities of both churches and recommend action to the following year's General Assembly.

2. Request the assembly to appoint an administrative commission to handle the reference from Hanover Presbytery.
3. Decline to hear the reference and return the matter to Hanover Presbytery without advice.
4. Decline the reference and return the matter to Hanover Presbytery with advice which deals more realistically with the human and ecumenical dynamics involved in it.

On June 12, 1970, Mr. Hart flew to Memphis from Richmond to present his brief to the judicial commission. He was shortly after joined by Dr. Mackenzie. It appeared unlikely that he would be invited to present his brief. While the standing committee was meeting behind closed doors, a friend passed out the ominous note: "Mac: Looks grim, but wait."

The standing committee continued to debate the question, seeking to find a suitable recommendation which the assembly would be willing to accept.

EXHIBIT 1

Letter from Ben L. Rose to Glenn Dickson

Lake Waccamaw Presbyterian Church

Box 146
Lake Waccamaw, North Carolina

Telephone: Manse 646-4101
September 23, 1969

The Reverend Glenn Dickson
St. Andrews Presbyterian Church
Broad Rock and Snead Roads
Richmond, Virginia 23224

Dear Glenn:
  I have your letter of September 10th and apologize for the delay. I do not have a secretary here and my correspondence has mounted.
  I shall try to answer your questions regarding the Ross MacKenzie case.

Delicate Matter

Whether the General Assembly has ever made a statement pertinent to this situation, I do not know. I can find no record of it in the books that I have here. You might write Jim Millard.

As for similar cases, I am told that Winston-Salem Presbytery not too long ago had a Negro minister who wanted membership in our Church and in a Baptist Church. Presbytery divested him of office. Also in 1963, William P. Burns was divested of office by Wilmington Presbytery because he joined the Episcopal Church. Look in the Ministerial Directory of our Church, 1967 edition, under William Parker Burns, you will find this note, "joined Episcopal Church, authority to exercise office withdrawn, Ap. 23, 1963, Wilmington Presbytery."

In my opinion, paragraph 111:3 of the Book of Church Order does apply to Dr. MacKenzie. According to that paragraph a minister, ruling elder, or deacon, may renounce the communion or authority of the Presbyterian Church in one of two ways. He may renounce it by (1) statement or he may renounce it by (2) joining some other Church. If he does either of these he renounces the communion or authority of our Church! According to this paragraph, the act of joining another Church is the act of renouncing. No statement is necessary. The act stands alone. The minister "renounces . . . by joining." Whatever his intentions or statements to the contrary may be, by joining he renounces! I think that is clear from the paragraph. In my opinion, it cannot be validly argued that this paragraph does not apply here. The intent of the paragraph is clear: joining another denomination is tantamount to renouncing the authority or communion of our Church. If we want to change the Book of Church Order to allow a man to hold membership in two denominations at the same time, let us do so. But let us not make the Book of Church Order say what it does not say, and let us observe what it does say! Under our present Book of Church Order, a minister may not hold membership in two denominations at the same time. That may be desirable, that is, it may be well to change the book so that we can encourage ministers to hold membership in several denominations at once, but the clear intent of the book at the present time is to forbid that. In his own mind, Dr. MacKenzie has not renounced the authority of the Presbyterian Church, but according to the Book of Church Order, he has!

I am glad that your commission is concerned to protect the integrity of the Book of Church Order, because I believe that that is where the greatest danger lies. Those of us whose hearts are with the ecumenical movement have sympathy for what Ross has done, but we dare not let that sympathy cause us to do anything that will jeopardize our ecclesiastical procedural safeguards. Our brethren of the Concerned Presbyterian camp would like nothing better than to weaken the authority of the Book of Church Order. The book is the rope that holds the Church together. We are not now bound by a single creed, or by a single aim, or by a single program. We are held together by our polity alone. And the Book of Church Order is that polity. If we want to become a congregational church, the first thing to do is to weaken the Book

45

of Church Order. *And that is what many of our ultra-conservative brethren want.*

One of the things that is happening in our Church right now is a loosening of the ties that bind the parts to the General Assembly (i.e., to the larger Church) and an increase of power at the congregational and presbytery level. If this is what is happening, and there is little doubt in mind that it is, then it will be even more necessary for us to take the Book of Church Order *seriously. Since the General Assembly will be taken less seriously, then the only thing that will hold us together will be the* Book of Church Order. *And if a presbytery can disregard its clear meaning, then we are in trouble. This is why I am so concerned to maintain the integrity of the* Book of Church Order *at this juncture of our Church's life. This is why Hanover Presbytery must take some action.*

And the only action that I see the Hanover Presbytery can take is to require Dr. MacKenzie to relinquish his membership in the Episcopal Church, and if he refuses then withdraw his authority to exercise his office in the Presbyterian Church. Presbytery might also overture the assembly to begin process to change the Book of Church Order *so as to allow dual memberships.*

May God guide your commission in its choosing. A great deal is at stake.

Sincerely,
(Signed) Ben L. Rose

EXHIBIT 2
Letter from Robert Gibson to Glenn Dickson

The Diocese of Virginia

110 West Franklin Street
Richmond, Virginia 23220   Telephone (703) 643-8451

Office of the Bishop
The Right Reverend Robert F. Gibson, Jr., D.D.

September 17, 1969

The Reverend Glenn Dickson
St. Andrew's Presbyterian Church
Broad Rock at Snead Roads
Richmond, Virginia 23224

Dear Mr. Dickson:
Your letter regarding the confirmation of Dr. Ross Mackenzie has reached me during a brief return to Richmond. I leave the country again

on September 18th and therefore, if you need help from my office on September 30th, I suggest that you call on Bishop Hall who is in charge during my leave.

In my intention and in my understanding in confirming Dr. Mackenzie, he did not renounce his membership or orders in the Presbyterian Church, nor did he become a member of the Episcopal Church. By his confirmation he did satisfy a technical legal requirement which then permitted me to license him to perform certain functions within the Episcopal Church.

I was hesitant about the act of confirmation precisely because of the ambiguity of denominational laws regarding membership and orders. I have high regard for membership and orders in the Presbyterian Church and in no sense wanted to dishonor or bring them in question.

It is difficult, if not impossible, to solve the problems of denominational law and discipline, and to act or think on a purely "Christian" basis. But this way my intention in this unusual instance.

In my understanding the theological meaning of confirmation is an invocation of God and Holy Spirit for the gift of strength to enable a Christian (a baptized member of the Body of Christ) better to fulfill the responsibilities of his membership. Surely Dr. Mackenzie did not need this beyond the grace and strength received in his Presbyterian ordination, but equally surely the invocation should not detract from spiritual strength already received. And I would argue that we all need as much renewed strength and prayer as we can obtain.

On a practical and legal basis confirmation has, of course, acquired other meanings within denominational practice. The most common one, from which the very name comes, is the adult confirming of baptismal vows made by sponsors in infant baptism. Adult confirmation for other than this purpose distorts this meaning, but has continued in practice because of the general exercise of infant baptism.

As a result of this, the Anglican Communion (of which the Episcopal Church is a part) has legally required confirmation in order to be a "communicant member" and Episcopalians do not receive Holy Communion until they are confirmed. This, as you know, was for long interpreted as barring non-Episcopalians from receiving Holy Communion in Anglican churches. Happily this has now been officially changed in Anglican interpretation.

But interpretation and change of canon law has still not caught up with the ecumenical situation. Although we provide for inter-communion of members, we do not yet provide for non-Episcopal clergy. The unhappy result is that Episcopal laymen can perform functions which are not legally open to Presbyterian clergy. And since the legal definition of eligibility was "to be confirmed" this became the legal loophole through which I could license Dr. Mackenzie to serve.

Frankly I am impatient about such laws clearly based on old denominational isolation. Perhaps it would have been wiser to ignore the law and simply ask Dr. Mackenzie to serve, but he preferred a legal approach. I can only trust that the well-intended act on his part and mine will in no way jeopardize his proper standing in the Presbyterian Church.

My warm regards,

Faithfully,
Robert Gibson

RFG:FBZ
Dictated by Bishop Gibson
but signed in his absence.

EXHIBIT 3
Letter from Ernest Thompson to Glenn Dickson

The Austin Presbyterian Theological Seminary
100 East 27th Street
Austin, Texas 78705

September 16, 1969

The Reverend Glenn Dickson
St. Andrew's Presbyterian Church
Broad Rock at Snead Road
Richmond, Virginia 23224

Dear Glenn:
In regard to the questions raised in your letter of September 10:
1. So far as I know no question has been raised regarding the confirmation of a PCUS minister in a Protestant Episcopal Church prior to the question as it is now raised by the recent confirmation by Dr. J. A. Ross McKenzie.
2. So far as I know the General Assembly has not expressed a specific opinion in the matter.
3. A somewhat comparable case arose in the 1960 General Assembly. A young minister was serving a church in West Virginia close to a small Episcopal church, without a rector, which had in its membership, as I recall, a number of scientists or technicians working on a government project. They were deeply religious men—but Anglo-Catholics—who wished to observe the Communion, but could not conscientiously receive it from the hands of a nonepiscopal minister. This young Presbyterian minister wished to receive supplemental ordination from an Episcopal Bishop, who was prepared to give it, in order that he might serve the Communion to these men. Greenbrier Presbytery overtured the General Assembly, asking if the Presbyterian minister might take Episcopal orders in order that he might serve both Presbyterian and Episcopal congregations.

The General Assembly answered this question in the negative for the reason that dual ordination is not provided for in our form of government and is contrary to presbytery doctrine. (GAM, 1960, pp. 24, 59; Digest, 1966, p. 103).

Confirmation of course is not ordination, but both, as you know, are regarded as sacraments by at least a portion of the Episcopal Church, and the confirmation in Dr. McKenzie's case and the ordination in the West Virginia case were intended to permit a Presbyterian minister to carry on certain services in the Episcopal Church that he could not do otherwise.

4. We recognize that the question of mutual recognition of ministerial order is a vital one in all ecumenical conversations, and is one which is not likely to be solved by the nonepiscopal minister having hands laid solely upon his head.

5. Formally BCO 111:3 does seem to apply to Dr. McKenzie's case. It seems to suggest that an officer renounces the communion or authority of PCUS by either a declaration to this effect, or simply by becoming a member of some other church—as I judge Dr. McKenzie has done in his act of confirmation. I doubt, however, whether the General Assembly and the presbyteries in voting this provision had any such situation in mind. There was no discussion at the time that I am aware of that would throw light on this question, but I presume what the fathers had in mind was the possible case where an officer would as it were, walk out of the Presbyterian Church by going off into another denomination.

6. Now the question has been raised I am inclined to agree with you and Mac that it would be wise to send up an overture to the General Assembly seeking some clarification of the issue, and/or some guidelines for future action.

I will not attempt to write the overture, but suggest that it might take one of two forms.

FORM ONE

Hanover Presbytery respectfully requests the General Assembly to give its interpretation of the Rules of Discipline Paragraph 111:3, specifically regarding the status of a minister in our denomination who has not renounced the communion or authority of this church (and does not intend to do so) but has become a confirmed member of the Protestant Episcopal Church, in order that he may preach more readily in its pulpit and have some part in the administration of the Lord's Supper in this congregation.

FORM TWO

Whereas, Rules of Discipline, Paragraph 111:3, was probably intended to describe only the case of a church officer who withdraws from the Presbyterian Church either by formal statement or by identifying himself with another congregation or church, and

Whereas, it does not therefore necessarily cover the case of a minister who does not renounce the communion or authority of this church, but who becomes a confirmed member of the Protestant Episcopal or other church in order that he may participate more fully in its life and practice while carrying on his ministerial responsibilities within this denomination.

Therefore, Hanover Presbytery requests the General Assembly meeting in Memphis in June, 1970

1. To advise whether there is any constitutional provision which prevents a minister of this church from becoming a confirmed member of a Protestant Episcopal or other church while continuing his full responsibilities as a minister in the Presbyterian Church in the United States.

2. To request the appropriate permanent or ad interim committee to study and report on the need and desirability of initiating conversations with the Protestant Episcopal Church and other churches, and/or making constitutional provision for some such mutual extension of ministry and ecumenical good will.

3. If the General Assembly answers this first question in the negative, then the step which Dr. McKenzie has taken is a significant one; if it responds affirmatively, as I think is likely, then it will have to be recognized that Dr. McKenzie's action was an irregular one. It will be generally recognized however, I think, that it was done in good faith; and therefore does not require disciplinary action. But it will become clear that it must not be taken as a precedent. The second request will give some support for Dr. McKenzie's intention, and may possibly (though I think this is very doubtful) lead to some constructive result.

I am sorry I am not in Richmond to talk with the two of you about the case. There may be aspects of the matter that I have not taken into account. There is no reason from my point of view why this letter or its contents should be kept in confidence.

> *Cordially and sincerely yours,*
> *(Signed) Ernest T. Thompson*

ETT/va

EXHIBIT 4

(The following statement which Dr. MacKenzie made to the Hanover Presbytery Commission on the Minister and His Work on September 30, 1969, was made an official part of the record of the Commission in its investigation of the matter of Dr. MacKenzie's relationship to the Protestant Episcopal Church. The statement as follows is a true and exact copy of the statement as made to the Commission and is so attested to by A. M. Hart, Stated Clerk, Hanover Presbytery.)

Statement of Dr. J. A. Ross MacKenzie
to Hanover Presbytery Commission on the Minister and his Work
September 30, 1969

The tragedy of which Czechoslovakia this morning is both a symbol and an instance is the failure to create a new pattern of life together. In every human community today the committed and the imaginative few are struggling painfully but hopefully to bring to birth new communities of meaning. Old political and social forms are being broken down in order that new ones may be raised up, and this process of renewal is a proof of the uniqueness of the human spirit. No human community has had clearer understanding of the ultimate source and justification of all renewal than has the Christian Church, whose God is not the utterly remote Being of Gnosticism but the Creator who constantly calls new worlds into being and the Savior God who has made a new creation in Jesus Christ.

This understanding has always meant for the churches of the Reformation that though the inner meaning of the Gospel can never finally change, all external forms have an impermanent character. It is, I think, historically true that the only times men have said that the church is dead have been those when inherited patterns were petrified and men forgot that the model of the people of God has always been that of a march or of a movement; never that of a settled political kingdom.

This is the essential insight of the church of the Reformation, condensed in the pregnant formula, *ecclesia reformata semper reformanda,* which simply means that God is the God of the new creation, creating new patterns of life together, humanizing static societies, bringing to birth new communities of meaning.

Whenever I go in the church I find that this is the irrefragable hope of countless men and women . . . but I also find mounting despair: despair that the church has grown old and tired and has lost the capacity for renewal; despair that the church has become like a flooded island cut off from the real life of men; despair that the church is preoccupied with legalisms and minutiae and unable to deal with the ultimate questions of human existence.

What is needed in our church is a sign that the hopes of many are not vain hopes; that the mood of the church can move from divisiveness to reconciliation and from despair to joy. In the first centuries of the church unity was above all things a unity of love; with the radical protest of the sixteenth century unity came to be understood as a unity of faith; can we conceive of the possibility that the Holy Spirit is calling us to move beyond ourselves into a unity of hope, in the process of which we shall even now cross over the lines of division that historical development has created into barriers and stumbling blocks, and even now seek at one another's altars and communion tables the remedy that Christ has provided for the healing of our brokenness?

On Ascension Day I was confirmed in St. Peter's Church, Richmond, by the Right Reverend Robert Gibson, whose untiring dedication to the cause of unity is as heartening as his courageous hopefulness that this act might be welcomed by both communities as an attempt to break down suspicions, not to raise them, and to build bridges, not to burn them. Since this act has caused no little concern and brought curious partners into alliance in condemning it, I seek now to explain and justify what I have tried to do.

1. *The meaning of confirmation.* There has been little constructive thinking about the meaning of confirmation in modern theologians, and there is

even greater confusion in some of my critics. Confirmation by the laying on of hands does *not* mean "joining the church." We join the church —though the phrase is a poor one—at baptism. Confirmation is rather a sign, indeed a means, of the giving of the Holy Spirit to those who have made a profession of faith and expressed a desire to serve the church or to serve human need through the church.

May the laying of hands be repeated? It may indeed, when one's own service or ministry becomes more specific. Paul, for example, at Antioch received along with Barnabas (Acts 13:3) a new laying on of the hands for the work to which the Spirit called them after he had earlier received the Spirit through the laying on of the hands of Ananias (Acts 9:17). The clear word of scriptures is that the laying on of hands may be repeated. Max Thurian says: "There is no theological objection to keep the imposition of hands, consecrating to a service, from being repeatedly given with different intentions on the part of the church" (Consecration of the Layman, page 84).

My confirmation, therefore, at the hands of Bishop Gibson I regard as something very like this: a commitment is a new kind of service in addition to the ministry which I exercise joyfully in my own sphere—it is a making of myself disposable to the will of God and available for the service of a particular Christian Community—in this case a small, black and Episcopal congregation—it is the giving of due and legal authority to serve that congregation. Such service will inevitably be limited, since clearly the greater part of my time will be given to what are at present my prior responsibilities.

2. *Confirmation by Christ and confirmation by the church.* In anger a friend of mine made this comment: "You have betrayed my church." On inquiring into his meaning, I learned that he considered my act to have called into question the validity of his baptism, confirmation, and ordination. No insult was or is intended; I do not have it in my nature to deride or push aside a ministry which I have sought to fulfill, I hope not without honor, for sixteen years.

It must be seen that there are two elements in confirmation or ordination: one spiritual, the other juridical. The spiritual element is that which Christ does once and for all in granting the Spirit, or for ministry; the juridical element is that which the church does in bringing a person under its care or discipline, in commissioning to some service, or in investing with authority. In our divided state this juridical element with the imparting of authority or commission has been given legal status. A Presbyterian has no authority to minister in a Methodist congregation since he does not have the authority by his own ordination. The problem, of course, is that by our division we have failed to allow the catholic nature of Christ's act to come into view.

It is no surprise to any of us that the historical church partakes of the relativity of history. What is needed is to break through these relativities, for to magnify our juridical authority is to make ourselves a sect.

I ask the question: Do you/we seriously mean it when we speak of the renewal of the church? And if we do, what as a public and demonstrable fact will the outcome of this renewal be? May it not be that some of us at least who have the privilege of sufficient time and the charism of the Holy Spirit will want to go out beyond the limits of our institutional forms to seek some kind of reconciliation over the barriers of color and class and denomination? I do not claim that what I have done is the next step for our church: but I do claim that we shall not know what the next step is or how we may make modifications so as to translate ecumenicity and catholicity into action unless someone takes that step.

A Delicate and Difficult Matter
B

The standing committee debated the recommendation of the Permanent Judicial Commission concerning the "delicate and difficult matter" of Dr. Ross Mackenzie's membership in the Episcopal Church. An amendment was proposed to the original recommendation:

The Committee recommends the following statement of the Commission be adopted: "THE COMMISSION RECOMMENDS THAT THE GENERAL ASSEMBLY DECLINE TO HEAR AND MAKE FINAL DISPOSITION OF THE REFERENCE OF HANOVER PRESBYTERY REGARDING THE CONFIRMATION AND LICENSING OF DR. J. A. ROSS MACKENZIE AS A LAY READER OF THE EPISCOPAL CHURCH." The Committee recommends that all advice and comment thereafter in the report of the Permanent Judicial Commission be deleted and the refusal to hear the reference be sent down without further advice or comment for the reason that further advice or comment may prejudice the work of the Inter-Church Relations Committee as it seeks to carry out the instructions of the General Assembly. (Vote: 13 for, 11 against.)

After debate, the amendment was approved by the Assembly.

Chapter 4
The United Parish in Brookline
prepared by Ann D. Myers

"Helping the homosexual is not like helping a crippled child, because helping a crippled child has a lot of appeal, but our cause does not." This statement was made to the Council of the United Parish (UP) Church at its meeting October 3, 1971, by Robert Jones, age twenty-six, director of the Homophile Community Health Service (HCHS), a recently established organization of approximately thirty people committed to providing psychiatric counseling and referral services to the homosexuals of Greater Boston. Under the agenda of new business the council was discussing a request by the HCHS for use of space in the UP Church. The homophile group had asked for a room for one of their counselors, the Reverend Donald B. McGaw, to counsel homosexuals during the day, plus a room large enough for a nine-person group therapy session on Wednesday evenings. In addition, the homophiles were requesting six rooms for three evenings a week for group therapy involving thirty to forty people. Earlier in the year, the group had solicited and received five hundred dollars from the UP.

As the council discussed the proposal at its October meeting, three general questions were raised. Two concerns about the availability of space and the possibility of extra work for the janitorial staff were voiced. The other issue centered around the propriety of possible contact between members of the HCHS coming for group sessions and "sensitive parishioners," in particular, the boys in the town's prospering Scout Troop. At the end of an unusually long meeting, the council voted to give

Mr. McGaw use of the building during the day for three-hour periods between nine and five for individuals only. However, council members expressed the desire for time to investigate the HCHS further before coming to a final vote on the proposal for large, evening group therapy sessions.

As Victor Scalise, age forty, and one of the three senior ministers in the UP saw the question, it was directly related to the major ethical stance of the church.

The Christian Ethic as people see it here is summed up very succinctly in the story of the Good Samaritan. The priest and the Levite pass by even though they see their countryman lying by the side of the road. But the Samaritan stops, because the man was in need of his assistance. And that is one fundamental question that has been raised now, "Do we help someone who is in need of our assistance or do we pass them by?" At the same time, there was a gut response to the effect of "We don't like this kind of individual."

Since both the ministers and the congregation of the UP believed that this ethical stance had to be validated through actions, one of the important issues confronting the UP was how it should structure its mission effort:

Sometimes there are practical questions which cloud the real issues—people can hide behind them. For instance, "We have x number of dollars; we have so much space. If we allocate space for this group, then we can't give it to someone else." This pragmatic approach is valid and at times it is difficult to discern when it becomes a red herring, an excuse not to admit the real gut response. At the same time, we do have to concern ourselves to some degree with the practical problems of mission. Currently we are debating how to structure our mission effort. Do we want mission to bring personal involvement to the church? Do we want to give money and space to people indiscriminately, or do we want to support certain groups to which we are sympathetic? I think we are leaning more and more toward a Good Samaritan approach—that we just don't want to support anyone who comes in off the street, but rather people who are in trouble. After all, we do have a lot to give. A large report which was just done on the United Parish indicated that even though we have more going on and more organizations in this church than in any other church in Brookline—perhaps in Boston, I've always wanted to say—the fact remains that we are still not utilizing our building to full capacity. To do this, I think, we first have to settle on what it means to be in mission here at the United Parish.

History of the United Parish of Brookline

The UP had been created in 1970 from the merger of three Brookline churches: the Baptist Church, the Harvard United Church of Christ, and St. Mark's United Methodist Church. All three churches were located within blocks of one another and were substantial in size. A suburb of Boston, Brookline had changed radically since World War II. The Yankee Protestant stock, which had been predominant in the town, had largely migrated to outlying suburbs, and by 1970 Brookline was approximately sixty percent Jewish. The population had grown increasingly transient, and the neighborhood had changed from a community of homes to one of expensive high-rise apartments. Lack of middle-income housing meant that it was difficult for young, less affluent families to locate in the town. Faced with the typical problems of the late sixties—falling attendance and dwindling finances—the ministers and key lay leadership of the three churches first met in 1966 to discuss merger possibilities. In his book, *Merging for Mission*,[1] Victor Scalise described the syndrome which they had organized to attack:

[All these sociological] factors [had] created a vicious circle. Fewer members meant less money and less money meant a reduction in ministries offered. A reduced capability for service resulted in fewer people. The whole process kept eating away at the morale of the congregations. Failure generated failure. Money for missions dwindled. In order for the church to survive, dollars were channeled into current expenses. Increasingly, the maintenance of the building, rather than the mission of the church, became the focus of the people and the pastor. Efforts turned from service to survival. All the churches were faced with similar problems. The community had become over-churched.

According to Scalise, the UP came into being because its initiators had made a crucial strategical decision. To avoid being trapped by what Scalise calls "building fundamentalism" or the tendency of mergers to get stymied over the reluctance of the congregation to give up its church building, this issue was dealt with at the very end of the planning period. In the begin-

[1] Valley Forge, Pa.: Judson Press, 1972.

ning stages, other questions, such as increased capability to minister to the needs of the congregation and community were discussed and commitment gained to these positive effects of the proposed merger. The forward momentum thus gained enabled opposition stemming from the "edifice complex" to be overruled.

Another decision made was to adopt a strategy of "escalation of tolerance." From the very beginning, each step was discussed with each of the congregations involved. During 1966–68, an Interchurch Planning Committee worked up broad support for the proposal; 1968–70 was a developmental phase during which time, activities were consolidated in the United Church of Christ building, a unified missions program begun, and the position of coordinating minister created. In April of 1970, all three churches at annual meetings, open to all members of the congregation, formally ratified the merger.

As a result, the participating churches lost approximately forty percent of their combined membership. In the fall of 1971, UP had eight hundred members officially on the rolls. Of that number, Scalise considered 303 families were actually pledging and active. Twenty-five percent of the 1970 membership had joined since 1965, and the majority of these were between the ages of twenty and thirty. However, forty percent of all those attending on a Sunday morning were over sixty years of age.

Two of the three churches had previously had a congregational form of government, while that of the third church was connectional. The government of the UP was representative. A council and five boards were responsible for making decisions. The bylaws made the council responsible for overseeing the total program of the parish, and stated that it should be "empowered to act for the Parish in all matters not specifically covered by the Bylaws, and not specifically reserved for Parish Meetings." This provision made the council the primary decision-making body in the church. According to UP bylaws, a quorum was defined as a majority or fifteen members of the council. The five boards were made up of nine members, three of which came from each church. These men and women served terms of three years. The five boards were designated as follows: Board of Spiritual Affairs, Board of Christian Education, Board of Christian Mission, Service Board, and Board of Business Affairs.

The United Parish Council was composed of twenty-eight parish members. While most were elected by the boards, a few came from the congregation at large. In the fall of 1971, this body tended on the average to be younger in age than those in the UP congregation. According to Donald Williams, age fifty and one of the parish ministers, this was due not to the lack of dedication to the endeavors of the church on the part of the older members, but rather to the fact that the younger parishioners had "more psychic energy available" than the elderly.

Almost half of the council members held or were working toward graduate degrees (M.A., Ph.D.). The older members of the congregation tended to be professionals—doctors, teachers—and businessmen. Also included were people such as Mrs. Raymon Eldridge, a woman in her mid-sixties, who was an ex-chairman of the council and had long been active in the official side of church life.

The Reverend Williams described the council as being "perhaps more liberal than conservative—by a small margin."

The current chairman of the UP Council was Dr. William Ensminger, age thirty, a medical student with a Ph.D. in microbiology. After several months' experience in his position, Dr. Ensminger felt that it would be beneficial to the decision-making process at the UP if more leadership could be exercised at the board level.

> The boards do not all function effectively. A limited number of people are capable of making these decisions that the boards are required to make. It would be great if each of the boards would do their job—then the council wouldn't have to deal with anything but the bigger issues. The boards waste a lot of time, and this is due in part, I think, to the chairman. In the case of the boards, leadership is very important in pulling things together and making decisions.

Ministry

The ministry of the UP was organized along horizontal rather than vertical lines. Each of the three senior ministers, who had been the ministers of the three churches, performed a special function. A Minister to Community for the UP was concerned with getting the congregation to express its faith through action groups. Groups centering around prison reform, housing and racial action had been formed under his direction. In addition, he had been involved in community groups, such as the Council for Planning and Renewal in Brookline and the Citizens' School Committee. As of fall, 1971, the UP was seeking a person to fill this post. The Reverend Victor Scalise held the title of Minister of Communication. One of his duties was to preach 50 percent of the Sundays, thus allowing the other ministers to devote more time to their responsibilities. In addition, Mr. Scalise coordinated the radio broadcast, "Music for Meditation," at 9:05 each Sunday morning on WCRB. He had also formed a number of small groups to "unite the congregation and expose them to the meaning of the Christian faith." Among these was a film workshop, the Jewish-Christian dialogue group, the contemporary Christian living group, and the person-to-person group which visited shut-ins.

The UP also supported a Minister of Teaching, the Reverend Donald Williams, who was essentially a nonteaching supervisor and was responsible for coordinating Sunday class sessions and overseeing the activities of student interns from the seminaries. Parish retreats and the church library were under his special care. According to an article on the UP "his other tasks included general parish ministries, as well as denominational, ecumenical, and community ministries." In 1971, he served as chairman of the town of Brookline's Drug Study Committee.

One of these three senior ministers served as a coordinating minister on a rotating basis.

Finances

One of the benefits and major reasons for the merger was to give the congregations and ministries of the three churches greater financial resources to redirect the church's mission. Eventually a steady income estimated at fifty thousand dollars per year would be provided by the sale of the Methodist and

Baptist properties. In 1971, St. Mark's Methodist Church was being rented by the Brookline school system for a yearly fee of twenty-four thousand dollars. In time, the building would be sold, and it was expected that income from investment of the proceeds would be approximately the same as the sum currently being received as rent. At the same time, the UP had entered into an option agreement with a real estate developer for the sale of the Baptist property. When the agreement was picked up, the sale made, and the money invested, the UP expected to receive yearly interest in the amount of twenty-five thousand dollars. In the meantime, the church was receiving a small monthly payment from the real estate firm to retain the option.

Victor Scalise felt that a trend that had existed in the past was likely to continue in the future, namely, that the pledging income of the UP would continue to be reduced, while the investment income of the church would increase. Heavy pledgers were usually older people, and, as members of this group died, they were not replaced by younger parishioners. According to Scalise, the younger group "generally had less financial commitment to the church, and more desire to buy material goods—cars, stereos, etc."

The Board of Business Affairs had projected a budget for 1972 of $155,344. This was a $20,000 increase over the 1971 figure (Exhibit 1). It was hoped that a sizeable portion of this increase could be spent for mission.

For the next few years, until the sale of both church properties had been finalized, Scalise felt that the church had to be careful not to get itself into an economic bind. On the other hand, he felt that excessive financial conservatism or a self-oriented outlook would atrophy the principle on which the parish was founded. He expressed the opinion in his article "Diversity in Unity," which appeared in the *Andover Newton Quarterly* in September, 1971, that the specialized ministry of the UP was a necessary factor in achieving the goals of the church.

The primary purpose of the United Parish in Brookline is mission. If we fail at this point, then we fail at all points. To come together for greater security or higher morale is not worthy of the Church of Jesus Christ. There must be a noble purpose. That purpose is to be in mission. Individually and collectively, we have a challenge to reach out. The uniqueness of what we have done is not in the projects themselves. Rather it is in the broad involvement permitted by a United Parish with a ministry of specialization.

The Homophile Community Health Service

An incorporated, nonprofit organization, the Homophile Community Health Service came into being early in 1971. With twenty-eight people on its staff, HCHS offered individual and group psychotherapy and pastoral and draft counseling to homosexuals. Most of the staff at HCHS were volunteers and worked a few hours each week. The HCHS had access to the services of three Ph.D. candidates in psychology, as well as several psychiatrists. Generally, the psychiatrists retained a supervisory position, advising the counselors or standing in as "recorders" of the events at the group therapy sessions. The regular counselors were usually people who had earned professional degrees in other areas. Among these were three psychiatric nurses, three or four social workers, and four pastoral counselors. The clergy were Catholic, Methodist, Unitarian, and Swedenborgian. All the clergy worked part time, but only the Catholic and Methodist were remunerated for their services. Robert Jones, head of HCHS, pointed out that, aside from being helpful in conducting regular counseling sessions, it was especially important to have these clergy on hand as consultants when a client was using his theology as a defense mechanism to hide himself from his problems.

In the fall of 1971, the HCHS was ministering to the mental health needs of more than one hundred homosexuals, a tenfold increase over the number they had started with at the beginning of the year. Approximately fifty new clients presented themselves for treatment each month, and many other homosexuals consulted the HCHS by telephone for information and/or referral to other agencies.

The service was involved in educating the larger community as well as coordinating the efforts of the homophile community toward self-help. Staff of the HCHS offered several courses on homosexuality in the Boston area: one each at Boston University Metropolitan College (night school), Tufts Experimental College, and the Cambridge Center for Adult Education (Exhibit 2). In addition, they were planning a seminar in the spring of 1972 for guidance counselors.

The HCHS was careful to define itself as an organization interested primarily in the mental health of homosexuals. Robert Jones felt that meetings with political or social overtones, such as consciousness-raising sessions, should be conducted by the various homophile social groups in Boston, and not by HCHS. However, one of the aims of the HCHS, according to Jones, was to promote community among homosexuals, and HCHS was willing to cooperate in making various homophile efforts in this area a success. Jones stated that there was little solidarity among the homosexual population and that in order for HCHS to meet the needs of its community, in a sense, it first had to create that community. In one step toward the creation of community, the HCHS sponsored the formation of a Community Advisory Board composed of twenty members, including the leaders of most of the homophile groups in Boston, medical personnel, as well as both clergy and laity. In another effort, HCHS was searching along with the Homophile Union of Boston and the Daughters of Bilitus (a female homophile organization) for an office building or series of store fronts, so they could locate in proximity to one another.

According to Jones, the biggest problem HCHS had was money, since it already had taken great steps in developing organization and administration and attracting clientele. In addition, a number of "space crises" had contributed to the inability of the health service to function smoothly.

The budget of the HCHS for 1971–72 (July 1 through June 30) was $58,588, of which approximately $50,000 was for salaries. However, not more than half the budgeted amount was actually spent, primarily because a large part of the services of the staff and all the office space had been given on a voluntary basis. Only five of the twenty-eight staff members were salaried, and these at only two-thirds of the budgeted amount, which generally amounted to one hundred dollars a week or less. While staff members received commissions, the total HCHS expenditure per week for this purpose was less than thirty dollars. A single volunteer on commission, such as an accountant, for instance, might receive twenty-five dollars per month. No staff member received fees directly from a client. Very little was spent on advertising, office equipment, supplies, or educational programs, since a large proportion of these were donated. Income derived from fees generally amounted to $350-$400 per week. In addition, two thousand dollars per year was obtained in grants from various private and public agencies.

During recent months the HCHS had been operating out of office space in the Church of All Nations building on Arlington Street, but had been forced to find temporary quarters at the Episcopal diocesan offices in Boston, since the landlord of the former building had decided to prohibit any ongoing activities during the evening hours. However, the Episcopal quarters were available only until January 8, 1972. Therefore, the HCHS requested space in the UP beginning January 10.

According to Robert Jones, the HCHS had approached the UP for several reasons. The first and most significant was the fact that, having been a seminarian himself, he felt most at home in the church. As a result, the HCHS had numerous contacts with churches in Boston, especially liberal ones, such as The United Methodist and Charles Street Unitarian. But as Jones pointed out, even the more staid churches had responded. Trinity Episcopal Church, for example, had given them three hundred dollars. Jones gave three basic reasons why he, as leader of the HCHS, had seen fit to approach the institutional church for so much of the service's support.

I think that one reason we approached the church was that that was where my contacts were. I was active in the church, and I knew the church—in the Methodist Church specifically, but also in other churches—so I felt very easy about relating to these people. The second reason we approached the church is that they are not as fiscally hung up as a foundation that has a lot of rules and regulations about how they give their money out. Church people are just people—if they have some money and they like what you are doing, they may just give it out without a great amount of deliberation. We felt we could relate more directly to them on a feeling level than we could, say, to a large foundation. And thirdly, we approached churches because churches are a major cause of the problem. Like other institutions, the church is interested in preserving itself and is, therefore, counter to anything that seems strange and new. I'm not sure the churches are *more* delinquent than the rest of society—I think all the institutions in society —government, business, church, are all into the societal bag together. They all feed into each other and keep each other anachronistic. The church just gets the blame because it vocalizes on morality and things like that, which in the case of homosexuals is very important, because the church is the mouthpiece for society's bad feelings about homosexuals. There are laws on the books, and medicine has chimed in with its opinion—all the institutions kind of play volleyball around whose responsibility it is to damn the queers. The laws on the books aren't very often enforced, and medicine is changing its views. There are very few doctors who will write treatises on the sickness theory of homosexuality anymore. But the church still has its rules on homosexuality, and I think a lot of people, because they were brought up in the church, relate more closely to the church than they do to something like law or medicine—because they had Sunday school teachers, their parents attended church, they have something that is much closer to a mother or a father feeling for the church. And then to have the church come out and say homosexuality is a sin, an abomination against God, that hits much closer to home than to have the laws of Massachusetts say that it is a lewd and lascivious act, or to have the doctors say we are sick. It hits people much harder. So one of the reasons we approached the church is because we feel it should be involved in the liberation of homosexuals.

First Contact with the HCHS

The UP's first contact with the Homophile Community Health Service occurred in the spring of 1971. Bob Jones had worked on a church project in South Boston with Dave Mitchell, a young UP member who was a Ph.D. candidate in social ethics at Boston University. Jones telephoned Mitchell one evening and told him he would like to ask the UP for a contribution to the HCHS. Dave Mitchell, who had informed Jones in a previous conversation that the prospects for obtaining help from the UP at that time were extremely slim, was surprised to have the subject come up again. Two programs, one for retarded children and another to raise the consciousness of the Brookline community on the issue of racism, had recently been the source of much controversy, and Mitchell felt that a request such as this one from the HCHS "would just blow the lid off everything." However, the ministerial staff unanimously recommended that Mitchell invite Jones to appear before the Board of Missions. Although the basic orientation of that board was traditional, still there were some who, according to Mitchell, were willing to consider "more *avant garde* mission programs," and it was for the benefit of these people that the staff felt the presentation should be made.

To Dave Mitchell's surprise, the Board of Missions labeled the HCHS request "an important one" and voted to take it to the council meeting on October 3. Mitchell was a member of the Social Concerns Group at the UP, which was composed largely of the more liberal element in the congregation. He felt that the aggressive stance that this group had taken on the issue of racism that year had evoked such negative response that they had decided to adopt a different strategy with respect to the HCHS.

It became quite clear to some of us after the Board of Missions took this open-minded stand on HCHS that we might have underestimated the flexibility of some of the more conservative leadership in the parish, because some of these conservatives sat on the Board of Missions. The consensus of our group was that Bob Jones ought to come in person with some of the key members of his staff to the April meeting of the council and make a polished presentation. Then we would see what would happen. In the meantime, the people in the Social Concerns Group decided that the best thing we could do was lay low and not identify ourselves with the project, because we had just passed the winter, at that point, in very antagonistic relationship with some of the leadership of the church over the racism project in the high school, and our image was distinctively negative, to the point where we had very strong feelings that if we made any positive push to support the homophiles, that would kill it. Therefore, we didn't invite anyone to our group to talk about it; we didn't initiate any educational programs.

On April 4, 1971, members of the staff of the HCHS made an appeal to the UP Council for monetary support for the newly established clinic. After handing out a report of their first two months' activities, three representatives of the HCHS endeavored to make the council aware of some of the reasons why an organization such as theirs should exist. They pointed out that

4.5 percent of the total population of the United States was homosexual and that approximately one in six of these were women. They explained that these homosexuals had many problems as the result of their treatment as a minority group. These included problems in securing and holding jobs, emergency housing, and family service. In addition, they pointed out that parents of homosexuals had problems of their own which they were often unwilling to discuss. In spite of the obvious need, there were no special provisions in the mental health facilities in the Boston area for treating the psychiatric needs of homosexuals. They explained that their project did have a religious dimension, in that they were receiving monetary donations and space from churches and that homosexuals often came to them with religious problems which were handled by the staff chaplain. At this time, the organization had two regular staff consultants and one nurse, who was handling records for several hundred patients as well as counseling individual patients. They felt that HCHS at that time was badly in need of money to support a secretary. This would be viewed as seed money only, since the organization aimed at being self-supporting.

After the HCHS had completed its presentation, it was proposed, for purposes of discussion, that the church donate one thousand dollars to the service. However, from the outset several council members felt this sum to be too high, and indicated that one half this amount would be sufficient. One influential member of the council, Mrs. Eldridge, felt that she would rather see the funds going to the Good-Will Inn for Boys in Dorchester, or a venereal disease and/or sex education program for youth of the church. The three senior ministers, when asked to give their opinion, spoke in favor of making a donation to the homophiles. Dave Mitchell, who was present at the council meeting, described the incident which, to his mind, had consolidated the council's support of the clinic.

Later on in the discussion, Dr. James Hobson, who is seventy-five and whom many of us in the Social Concerns Group had identified basically as being very conventional in his missions orientation, stood up and in essence gave a ringing endorsement of the proposal. He said he had in his capacity as a school psychologist in the Brookline school system had a great deal of experience with the problems that homosexuals had to deal with, and he was aware of the fact that they were ostracized and had real difficulties getting help from the conventional psychiatric profession. This was essentially a reiteration of what the people making the presentation had said, but coming from a member whose credentials were impeccable in terms of the more conventionally oriented people on the council, it was the straw that broke the camel's back. After he made his statement, a number of people who had been on the fence and who had been nervous about talking about the whole thing anyway had their attitude definitely changed—at least toward a stance of nonresistance, if nothing else.

Dave Mitchell also felt that the participation in the HCHS presentation of a qualified doctor from the Boston University Medical Center had stood the organization in good stead. In general, most of the council members as well as the ministers were favorably impressed with the information they had received and the way in which it had been imparted. At the end of the meeting, the council voted to contribute five hundred dollars to the HCHS.

Robert Jones felt that in approaching various organizations for support, it was incumbent upon the HCHS to communicate to the best of their ability the objectives and needs of the health service. In order to do this, Jones felt it was necessary to modify each presentation to fit the specific group being approached. When talking to a member of the Boston financial district Jones employed the financial jargon, and used the frame of reference of psychiatrists when addressing a mental health group. This tactic, he felt, served to contribute to the understanding of the health service and eliminate a certain number of semantic blocks.

He pointed out that they had avoided speaking in any way at the UP which might make them seem unduly militant:

We avoided using the words "gay liberation" because the term "liberation" carries with it all sorts of other connotations today. But we did talk about human suffering and the psychiatric profession and how we are a part of the professional mental health community. Some of the people on the parish council are doctors—I think the new chairman is, for instance—and a lot of them are professionals. They can relate to a professional approach.

Here is a case in point about the importance of words: we do "marriage counseling" at HCHS, but we have learned to call it "couple counseling" instead of marriage counselling, because churches get very uptight when you talk about marriage counseling for same-sex couples. One church accused us of performing marriages, because we have ministers on our staff. So we have to drop the term "marriage" from our terminology, except when we are talking about bona fide heterosexual couples. In general, during an interview, we listen to questions and try to answer the questions people are asking, and not talk a lot, because that gets you into trouble.

In our presentations, we don't avoid saying what we feel to people. However, we are just very good with words. Our formal objectives —which we stressed in our interview with the United Parish—are to provide informed sympathetic counselling and referral for homosexual men and women. Beyond that, our general objective is the eventual change in life-styles—at least tolerance and acceptance on the part of the larger community that homosexual life-styles are viable alternative life-styles.

Members of the HCHS also made sure to dress in a way that would not offend the group to which they were speaking. Robert Jones, for instance, stressed the fact that he always wore a coat and tie when making an appearance at the UP.

Council Meeting—October 3, 1971

When Robert Jones returned on October 3 to solicit space in the UP for individual and group therapy sessions, he and his staff again made a positive impression on the council. William Ensminger, chairman of the council at the time, expressed the feeling that it was Jones's manner, as much as anything, that had moved the council members.

One week before the council meeting, I got a letter from Jones outlining his request for space. My immediate reaction was that it was excessive for any group to ask to use six or seven classrooms in the church building three nights a week. However, on Sunday afternoon, I called several people on the council who were middle-of-the-roaders and told them of Jones's request. Their reaction was "Well, we gave them five hundred dollars. Why should we do more? This is too much." I called Bob Jones to see if the HCHS was applying to other places and said that we couldn't give three nights, but could possibly swing one night. I did say there was a strong conservative element in the church that would have to be placated. That night Jones came to the council meeting and had to wait for 1½ hours before he came in. What was very impressive was that he recognized and was sensitive to the fact that we had been in the meeting a long time (it was 9:00 or 9:30 P.M.), and he didn't take very long, and he didn't give us a prepared speech. He was obviously a dedicated, intelligent guy whom most people would be willing to trust. If he had turned out to be high pressured or even a neurotic himself, he wouldn't have gotten anywhere with the council.

The council finally voted at that meeting to allow the Reverend Donald McGaw to hold counseling sessions during the day, plus one nine-person therapy group on Wednesday evenings. They decided to postpone the discussion of whether or not to permit the homophiles to hold group sessions of thirty to forty people, three nights a week, until the next council meeting. Marion Jacobsen, wife of the UP's "house radical" (Stephen Jacobsen, Ph.D. candidate in Physics at Northeastern University) and a candidate for a master's degree in education, volunteered to write a report in the meantime and investigate the three main areas of concern to the council: the HCHS itself, the need for janitorial services, and the availability of space.

Use of Space in the United Parish: Mission

The request of the HCHS required the members of the UP Council to struggle with the definition of mission at the UP. Part of the question involved priorities for the allocation of resources such as space.

Existing regulations for the use of space in the UP were broad in scope (Exhibit 3). Organizations, both church-related and those external to the church, used space on both an occasional and a regular basis. Among the groups using or requesting to use space in the church during the fall of 1971 were the Boy Scouts of Brookline, the Brookline Women's Club, and Alanon, a group for the families of alcoholics (Exhibit 4). Parish policy was to charge those groups which it felt could pay, and then the fee was usually only large enough to cover janitorial services. However, if a group were interested in using a large hall, they were required to pay for heating and electricity. On October 3,

1971, the Parents Without Partners, Inc., Boston Chapter, requested use of the UP's spacious Willett Hall and adjacent kitchen facilities for a children's Christmas party on Sunday, December 12, from 1:00 to 5:00 P.M. The UP decided to charge Parents Without Partners fifty dollars for the use of these facilities. Victor Scalise felt that policy on use of space was a good one.

In my opinion, the fees we charge are quite modest. We are a service organization and want to provide service to the community—we cannot earn money, because we would be liable to taxation. Who gets charged, however, is entirely up to the boards and the council. For instance, we have made a conscious decision that the Boy Scout troop is such a worthy cause that we are willing to absorb their costs. Similarly, we are going to underwrite a Black Respect Day, which black students at the local high school are planning. We're saying to the kids at the school, "We want to help you get started and know you don't have money, so we will help you out." But we charged Parents Without Partners, because we know they have money.

Dave Mitchell had no quarrel with the UP's regulations for use of space. However, he, along with Marion Jacobsen, tended to see mission as a total commitment of resources. Mitchell had been a member of St. Mark's United Methodist Church prior to the merger and said he had watched a preoccupation with the internal operation of the church, specifically maintenance tasks and "compatible, close fellowships," result in a vitiation of the church's engagement in mission. "We became," he said, "like a grease factory with no shipping department. We were using all the grease to keep the machines going." Consequently, Mitchell felt that in order to avoid getting into this rut, the UP building should be used as much as possible. This was necessary he felt, both to add vigor to the mission effort and simply from the practical standpoint that maintaining such a large structure involved considerable overhead expense and that this investment should be capitalized upon.

It's stupid to have a Cadillac and not drive it because the gas costs too much. We've got a building which we're spending twenty or thirty thousand dollars a year to maintain, and we're using it less than twenty percent of the time. Eighty percent of the money that we use to run that building is being wasted because it is being used to keep the building at sixty degrees and to hire janitors to dust and mop rooms which simply aren't used. Now that's stupid, I think. And it's not a question of missional priorities; it's a question of plain common sense. My solution is to go outside and find people who will use it. They can pay for the space if they are able, and, if not, we will donate it. But the biggest problem will be getting this point across to a significant number of people in the leadership that the question is not one of priorities, but of utilization. If the utilization figure got up to sixty or seventy percent, then we could start talking about priorities.

Another problem is that some people desire activities in the church to remain on a small scale. A statement Mrs. Hobson made last year on this issue is symbolic of the way a lot of people tend to feel on this. A request was made to Mr. Scalise by the Children's Museum for space for four days in the church (by-laws required that the final decision be made by the UP Council), so he called a few people, including Mrs. Hobson. Her response was, "I just think there are too many things going on here now. There is so much going on, I can't keep track of it all." Well, my reaction to that is, if you are at the point where you can't keep up with it all, you should try to localize your involvement so that you can keep up with what you personally are involved in. But don't hold the church back just because you are slowing down. But I think her response represents the feeling of a lot of people in the leadership and elsewhere. And to use that criteria means to continue to have that building unutilized eighty percent of the time, because that's how it's being used now, and they feel there is too much going on.

Mr. Stokes, age sixty-three, a vice-president in the New England Telephone Company and a member of the UP Council and Board of Business Affairs, was not so sanguine as Dave Mitchell about the ability of the church to give freely of its resources. He, like many of the older members, felt that since the UP had been created at the expense of a part of the membership of each church involved, and now had to support three ministers, that it was under some financial strain. Stokes felt that, given the monetary situation in the UP, he should not be called upon to donate money or space to groups which might be capable of paying their own way. He placed the HCHS in this category.

I think that you have to keep in mind that we have had trouble keeping the UP economically viable. My feeling is that if we do go down the homophile road, then we are simply a second United Fund. We have certain facilities which have become ours by inheritance, and here some group sits, parceling it all out. I don't believe most people belong to a church in order to have that happen. However, irrespective of the reasons for church membership on the part of the public, I'll just keep to economics. I personally tithe. If I take what I give to the United Fund and to this church from my net income, I tithe. As I see the system, I would rather give the money to the United Fund than to a little group here which is deciding that it is going to pass out the assets of this church on the basis of applications.

Furthermore, I don't think that homosexuals fall in the same class as welfare recipients, though it is true that they may have some problems psychologically in recognizing that they are not accepted. Two fine young ladies related to me each married sailors, and when these sailors came back from the navy, they were homosexual. Well, one of them is making fifteen thousand dollars and the other eighteen thousand dollars a year. Why should the church be giving money or donating space to people making that kind of money? These homosexuals do have problems—both marriages that I am speaking of have broken up. But it isn't like the poverty-stricken or those in nursing homes who have no assets to build their own lives. My personal opinion is that priority at the UP should be given to those people who have no one else to turn to.

Robert Jones himself recognized that to become fully established as an ongoing organization the HCHS would have to be able to support itself. In the meantime, the service had to rely on the beneficence of those who were sympathetic to the plight of the homophiles. At the time the HCHS was looking for money from three sources: foundations, the government, and the homophile community itself. The third category, the homosexual community, would ostensibly be the most reliable and continuous source; however, Jones indicated that there were difficulties in counting on affluent homosexuals to donate funds.

The problem in seeking money from the homophile community is this: the people in the community who have money are very hidden. They are secretive, because of the fears they have of losing jobs, families, and friendships. The homosexual is basically invisible and is able to hide. This is particularly true of "gay" people with money —they have built up huge defenses around them. And that's why we have problems. We deal mainly with the lower income group —students, young people, not the clients who can afford to hire a private therapist at high rates. The only foundation grant we have received to date came from a foundation that only had two hundred dollars to give away. They gave us the two hundred dollars, and written in on the letter by the man who was responsible for giving away the money was a suggestion: "Why don't you use this money to put out a brochure to reach monied 'gay' people?" Well, we have been so short of money that we haven't been able to spend it that way, but we are definitely considering that strategy for the future.

Attitudes Toward the HCHS: Mission

A basic concern of many people in the parish was whether the HCHS was the type of organization that they would like to see associated with their church. Some people acknowledged that their feelings about the church's involvement had to do with their attitude toward homosexuality. Many of the older members in particular found it difficult to change the negative associations they had built up for most of their lives. Mr. Stokes summarized the feelings he saw his peers wrestling with:

The people of my age group and experience who have talked to me about this have a thesis something like this: homosexuals are perverts; perversion is not something that the church should encourage. Even though some group—i.e., the UP Council—has decided they are going to encourage perversion, these people would prefer not to be associated with a group that is going to encourage perversion. The average person in this church doesn't know whether homophiles are mentally ill, good or bad, but the morality in which these people were brought up is that you don't encourage this particular activity. And their attitude is, let's not talk about it.

Dr. James Hobson, age seventy-five, a psychologist and a member of the council, had been coordinator of personnel services in the Brookline public schools for thirty-four years and a consultant for various projects, such as the College Entrance Examination Board and the Brookline Health Department. He expressed a sympathy with the problems of homosexuals, but also some reservations about their use of the UP facilities.

I have in a few instances during my career been called upon to counsel homosexuals. The problem has assumed a magnitude, particularly in the public eye in recent years much greater than it ever did in the past. Homosexuals have always been the lepers, the pariahs, of society and at the same time have been individual human beings with great problems and among the most miserable of human beings. And it is from that point of view that I feel the church should attack the problem. I spoke in favor of the church contributing to the society, and I spoke in favor of allowing individual counseling to go on in the church. However, I am against allowing several groups of homophiles to meet in the church. I feel that this is a logical position in that I am a psychologist, but I feel I'm also a practical person in that it doesn't pay to create more problems than you solve. We have in this church the most famous Boy Scout Troop in New England. The same man has been Scout Master since 1925 and has devoted his life to it. He has turned out a record number of Eagle Scouts. I am in favor of our dealing with the homophile problem, but I don't want to see the UP Church become the gathering place for homosexuals and have that reputation. I feel that this would prevent parents from allowing their boys to join the Boy Scouts.

And I think I feel that there is something else to be considered here. This is a parish of three churches and largely a parish of old people —most old people are horrified at the idea of homosexuality. And this is what I mean. I don't think that in a parish which is to come together that it pays to try to introduce a factor which will lose members even if it's a few older members. I think that a person who has belonged to a church and expected certain things from it has a right to die with the church still fulfilling certain things that he expected. Now it's true that the modern churches need to do a lot of things that churches didn't use to do, and you cannot make a spiritual living by taking in each other's religious washing. That's why I think we have to have more outreach than we have, and we have to have more doing and less talking.

Most of the liberals in the congregation felt that homosexuals coming for therapy would be discreet and inoffensive to any members of the congregation they might encounter. Most of them agreed to support the HCHS on the basis of the rationale Marion Jacobsen expressed in her report:

It should be noted that homosexuals are not distinguishable in appearance from heterosexuals and that there are occasionally both homosexuals and heterosexuals whose public display of sexual behavior is objectionable, but that this is such a rare occurrence that it does not need to be considered as a serious possibility in these circumstances. A letter has been received from the Reverend Bradford Bryan, Pastor of the Church of All Nations, indicating that they have encountered no difficulty in this matter, in spite of their location in an area of the city that attracts a significant number of homosexuals. Also, contact between clients of HCHS and members of our parish will be limited by the fact that the building receives little regular use (only choir rehearsal and monthly board meetings) at the requested times. The nature of the activity (scheduled counseling sessions), and the fact that the HCHS office, where initial contacts are made, will remain at the Church of All Nations insures that there will be no tendency for the parish to become a congregating place for large numbers of homosexuals. It should be noted also in this context that the groups being considered are for psychotherapy, and so are not in any sense social gatherings.

Most UP liberals also supported the orientation of the HCHS which was that of treating the emotional or mental adjustment of their clients rather than their homosexuality. Dave Mitchell felt that he could stand up for the rights of homosexuals to lead the kinds of lives they desired, but that he wasn't sure if he could adjust to being in close contact with the "gay" subculture.

I was taught like everyone else that homosexuality was weird and nasty, etc., but I personally would say at this point that I have no difficulty affirming the right of a homosexual to be free of harassment. I would say that this attitude doesn't make it any more comfortable for me to be in a situation in which this is a very common manifestation. There is a point, I think, beyond which diversity in life-styles is very difficult to blend, and it may be necessary for people to make conscious decisions to minimize their routine contacts because neither one of them can adjust to the life-style of the other. Now, in this case, it may be one-sided. It may very well be that "gay" people are more able to adjust to the heterosexual life-style than the other way around, but I think that is something that our society has to work out in the future.

Notwithstanding my general support of HCHS activities at our church, and my feeling of the need for liberation of homophiles, I wouldn't find myself going to a "gay" dance to show my solidarity in the way that I might be willing to go to some function to show my solidarity with the blacks. Psychologically, I'm just not prepared to step that far out.

Victor Scalise felt that his own instinctive response was one of repulsion at the idea of homosexuality. However, he went on to say that the only stance which he could validate as a Christian and a minister committed to mission was that of a compassionate helper. For this reason, he felt that the UP should contribute space in the church to the homophile society.

The case-writer asked Mr. Scalise how he viewed statements such as those made in a bulletin by the Lutheran pastor of Arizona State University in the spring of 1971 (Appendix A) affirming the fact that he intended to "hold fast to the Scriptures" as his "final court of appeal" on the morality of homosexuality. In the bulletin, the campus minister quotes Romans 1:24-27: "They gave up God and therefore God gave them up—to be the playthings of their own foul desires in dishonoring their own bodies . . . the men, turning from natural intercourse with women were swept into lustful passions for one another. Men with men performed these shameful horrors, receiving, of course, in their own personalities the consequences of sexual perversity."

Scalise responded that he felt strongly that he was justified in downplaying pronouncements of this type and in elevating the concept of the Good Samaritan to one of prominence in the UP:

Most people today are biblical illiterates—they don't know their Bible and would not draw on biblical authority. The Bible does not have authority for most people. But if by some chance a person would come to me with some passage from the Bible, I guess I would say the same thing that I would say about the book, *Merging for Mission,* which I have just written. I would make no attempt to justify and defend sentences and paragraphs out of context, but I would defend what can be called the spirit. And it is quite clear to me that the message of the Bible and the Christian faith is one of compassion—everywhere I see Jesus concerned with helping those people who are the outcasts, the sinners, who have suffered crippling diseases, be they emotional or physical. I mean the whole message of the gospel is to redeem and save those that are the lost. And if we aren't about that, then we aren't about the Christian faith.

This, of course, is a basic biblical argument: "Do you accept what you want to accept and reject those things that you want to reject?" Well, yes! Yes. Martin Luther did it—he said that certain books in the Bible were only good enough to be thrown into the sea. People have always done that. Not only would I be selective because certain passages are vindictive and hateful and mean, but because you have to sort out the cultural message as opposed to the religious message. Biblical authority today is shallow, because there are not many people equipped to deal with these issues in an honest intellectual fashion.

After all, there is not a person with any sense in his head who thinks that the world is flat or that it's a seven-tiered world. The Bible is not a book of biology or archaeology, and I would not try to defend anything in it of a scientific nature. But I would defend the religious principles of the Bible which I think are well taken.

As far as homosexuality goes, I don't think myself, and some doctors will tell you this, that it is an emotionally healthy reaction. However, I am acting in accordance with what I think is that Christian message —the Bible teaches that the Christian message is compassion.

Interim Occurrences

Prior to the meeting of November 14, Marion Jacobsen's report outlining in detail the finances, organization, and philosophy of the HCHS was made available at the UP library. Marion Jacobsen and Dave Mitchell had asked William Ensminger to visit the HCHS himself. Being a medical student, William had no time to give to such an investigation. However, since he felt that the sensitivity of some of the HCHS supporters to the types of issues the congregation was concerned with was rather low, he felt he would like someone "more conservative and rational" to look into the service. Accordingly, he requested that Victor Scalise undertake this task. Mr. Scalise spent an hour talking with Bob Jones at the HCHS headquarters and produced a brief supplementary report which he felt would be helpful to the council in coming to a decision. These included a list of the churches in the Boston area presently contributing space and/or money to the health service and some comments on the way in which homosexuals would be referred to the meetings and therapy sessions at the UP. Bob Jones was impressed with the way in which Mr. Scalise had handled the visit.

I think the most interesting and straightforward kind of contact I had with the UP was when Victor Scalise came here, and he and I had a long talk. He just leveled with me at one point and said he had received calls saying that if the UP continues to support homosexuals, some people will leave the church. He said he had been through that process before and related the incident when they had an organist whom some families didn't like. Other families, however, said that if he fired the organist, they would leave. Faced with the fact of losing four families, they nevertheless released the organist. Victor said, "If it looks as if we are going to lose too much money and too many leaders because of your coming in to use space, then I will oppose it."

Political Situation Prior to November 14

Council members were to vote November 14 on whether to allow the large group therapy sessions use of six rooms in the church for three evenings a week. It was difficult to tell how the decision would fall. This was in part due, Dave Mitchell said, to the nature of political interaction at the UP.

With most issues here at the UP, there hasn't been any regular systematic attempt to politicize in terms of trying to line up the people and say, let's count the votes. And I think that has been healthy in one sense, because it has meant that council decisions are relatively free and open, with the exception of the fact that people are keenly aware of the fact that there is a broad spectrum of theological orientation about the nature of the church and what it really is and what it's supposed to be doing. There are sort of patterned reactions to the way people say things. You catch yourself saying, "Oh well, you'd expect her to say that." But still, there is a propensity for the discussion to stay somewhat open, rather than having things decided before the meeting. More than one person has commented to us about that, saying that it's kind of unusual, because so many people who are used to working in group situations are accustomed to walking into a meeting where the leadership has essentially lined up people to vote the way it wants and everything is all set.

Liberals felt that even though the homophile request might be defeated in the end, just the chance to bring such an issue to some of the more conservative parishioners' attention might be positive influence. They felt it was important to involve all members of the congregation actively in mission, and that a situation should be avoided which would allow the more liberal element (10 percent of the membership) to form their own private crusades. Dave Mitchell commented:

We feel that we must take seriously the social problems of the city around us and that one of the ways to do that is simply not to talk theoretically about this, but to have concrete proposals presented to the parish at regular intervals, which the parish then has to deal with. In other words, they are faced with a concrete decision; it's not an abstract or theoretical discussion, but a pragmatic problem, and they have to respond yes or no, and they have to decide why. It is very important to open up the thinking of the people about what it means to be in mission, and the only way you are going to do that is face them with a concrete situation, because otherwise the avoidance tendencies are too great. People get into the mission study syndrome. They go through the four-week packages where all the experts come in and tell you what it means to be in mission, and they have a nice enjoyable experience and warm their hearts a bit, but nothing really changes. And when it comes to deciding how the budget's going to be constituted and how the building's going to be used, the decisions are the same as they always were.

The chairman of the council, William Ensminger, had decided to support the HCHS, but was extremely nervous about what the conservative members of the congregation might be feeling.

Each person of a conservative bent who is supporting this organization, and this includes myself, does so at the risk of developing a fair amount of hostility to it. We are taking a chance, because we have already been warned that some people are thinking of leaving the church. Those who are sensitive to the congregation have gone against their better judgment. Personally, I am afraid that there may be overstepping by the homophiles, such as publicity that the UP is a counseling center.

Mr. Stokes felt that people had not been given enough time to adjust to the idea of the church offering its charity to homosexuals. He described how his company had made an effort six years previously to hire blacks and had initially met with much resistance in first stages of trying to implement this policy.

It took us six years to make any headway at all. And that's the trouble with this situation in the UP—they are trying to introduce something very, very controversial too fast. To deal with this black situation at the telephone company, we made a film—it took us a year. We ordered every single management person to see the film, and then we discussed it for two hours. And we had a different situation. Everyone in this organization has an automatic veto. If I don't happen to like homosexuals flocking to my church, I can leave and suffer no penalty. Now when you are working and decide to quit, you suffer a real penalty—your salary. So it seems to me that there is a charge here against the church and the ministers to recognize this situation.

Victor Scalise was aware of the sentiment opposing the HCHS and wondered how it would affect the UP fund drive, which had been scheduled for the afternoon of November 14. He said he had heard of one man, a business executive and vice-president of one of the largest firms in town, who had succinctly voiced his intention—"If they come in, I go out." The ministers of the UP were all planning to be on hand the afternoon of the fourteenth to man the telephones in case the canvassers encountered any questions or complaints which they thought should be passed on.

Scalise had one strategy up his sleeve which he had not yet put into effect full force, primarily because he did not feel that the issue was something that he cared to give total commitment.

If I felt this were something that the church would stand or fall on, I would call on every single individual that I knew in his home. Personally, I would sit down with every one of them, and just try to be a friend, and ask, "How do you feel about this issue?" I would let them unburden their feelings, and then I would try to indicate as best I could that I understood how they felt. In short, I would work with them, as I did with the Baptists on the issue of forming the UP (and the Baptists voted unanimously for the merger).

There is nothing, absolutely nothing, that can beat personal contact with your key people, and some of them may not be people in elected positions. I know a woman who is on the phone all day long—I don't mean that negatively—and I know that if I have that woman with me, I can be sure it will be an influence for the good. And I see that woman a couple of times a month, and that's more than I see a lot of people, but I know the kind of influence she has and the kind of people she touches. So I call her. And an hour's visitation and sipping tea in her home some people would call a waste of time. But if anyone is ill, I get a call from her. And if she knows about any kind of rumble, I know about it and can go and defuse it, before anything starts to happen. I can say I have many weak points in my ministry, but this is one of my strong points. And I would say that this is the way to deal with such things: Don't come in like a bull in a china shop.

Both groups in the church feel that the decisions at the board meetings and in the council fall to the other faction. The liberals think that no decisions are made in their favor and the conservatives feel just the opposite—that people involved in the community get everything they want. It's very interesting that they don't listen to one another—don't talk to one another. Both groups are threatening to leave the church or cut off their money, because they aren't getting their way. So you really have to be a reconciler and healer. I see my role as one who is to bring continuity and reconciliation among the people of the church. Often that means you get flak from each group because you choose to identify with neither one. This may happen over the HCHS.

EXHIBIT 1
The United Parish of Brookline
Preliminary 1972 Budget

Summary

Expenditures

Program	Spending	Overhead Alloc. (Preliminary)	Total	
Spiritual affairs	$ 34,333	$16,710	$51,043	(33%)
Community	34,347	12,100	46,447	(30%)
Communication	16,830	2,305	19,135	(12%)
Christian education	7,340	24,200	31,540	(20%)
Service	4,874	2,305	7,179	(5%)
Overhead	57,620			
Total	$155,344		$155,344	

Income

Endowment	$ 28,500	
Plate	3,000	
Special offerings	1,050	
Rental	26,448	
Use of bldg.	1,180	
Pay phones	265	
Subtotal	$60,443	
Req'd. pledges	94,901	13% Increase
Total	$155,344	

The United Parish of Brookline

Preliminary 1972 Budget

Program Expenditures

Program	Total	Salaries	Benev.	Expense Categories			
				Material	Program	Maint.	Other
Spiritual Affairs	$ 34,333	$32,973	...	$ 460	$ 400	$ 500	...
Worship	19,535	18,575	...	460	...	500	...
Calling, counselling	12,898	12,898	...	...	...	...	...
Young adults	1,900	1,500	...	...	400	...	...
Community	34,347	6,227	28,120	...	...	...	...
Missions, outreach	27,620	...	27,620	...	...	...	...
Ministry	6,727	6,227	500	...	...	...	...
Communication	16,830	10,930	...	1,400	2,800	...	1,700
Ministry	3,168	2,668	...	...	500	...	...
Parish news, radio, etc.	13,662	8,262	...	1,400	2,300	...	1,700
Christian Education	7,340	4,490	...	1,150	1,700	...	...
Church school	2,350	1,120	...	1,150	...	...	...
Early service	2,400	2,400	...	...	...	...	...
Parker Hill	300	...	...	...	300	...	...
Ministry, camp, etc.	2,290	890	...	...	1,400	...	...
Service	4,874	1,334	2,844	96	600	...	...
Dinners, coffee, etc.	246	...	...	96	150	...	...
Denominational admin.	4,628	1,344	2,844	...	450	...	...
Overhead	57,620	31,911	107	2,900	...	19,822	2,880
Building	34,812	12,640	...	2,350	...	19,822	2,880
Local admin.	22,808	19,271	107	550	...	...	...
Total	$155,344	$87,865	$31,071	$6,006	$5,500	$20,322	$4,580

The United Parish of Brookline Budget
Three-Year Comparison, 1970–72

	1970 Actual	1971 Budget	1972 Current Exp.	Budget Benevolence
Ministries:	$ 40,476	$ 43,191	$ 42,825	
Salaries		27,100	28,836	
Retirement		3,456	3,218	$1,650
Housing		6,000	5,775	
Car		3,700	3,700	
Insurance		1,180	1,296	
FICA		1,755		
Christian Education:	7,820	5,150	5,650	
College		200		
Youth		200		
Adult		200		
Materials		400	1,150	
Supplies		200		
Equipment		150		
Summer		200	300	
Camps		500	600	
Staff		3,100	3,600	
Young Adult:		1,900	1,900	
Intern		1,500	1,500	
Program		400	400	
Staff:	27,892	28,756	27,856	
Secretaries		14,979	15,970	
Custodians		11,402	11,886	
Benefits		2,375		
Denominational:	3,165	4,274	4,602	
St. Mark's		3,174	3,352	2,304
UCC, Baptist		800	800	9,535
Conventions		300	450	
Operating:	25,983	16,200	22,400	
Fuel	6,320	4,500	5,620	
Utilities	3,172	1,900	3,060	
Telephone	1,493	1,700	1,500	
Insurance	6,394	3,600	7,870	
Maintenance	8,604	4,500	4,350	

Three-Year Comparison (cont'd)

	1970 Actual	1971 Budget	1972 Current Exp.	Budget Benevolence
Music:	9,258	9,500	9,760	
Organist		$ 3,300		
Asst. organist		715	$ 4,170	
FICA		155		
Choir		5,250	5,510	
Music		80	80	
Subtotal	$114,594	$108,971	$114,993	$13,489
Dinners	1,373	500	246	
Housekeepers		900	754	
Office exp.	3,256	3,000	3,185	
Equipment	169	1,500	1,725	
Advertising	894	1,200	1,100	
Radio	1,240	1,200	1,200	
Funds		1,500	1,500	
Council		500		
Ministries		1,000	1,500	
Audit	200	200	200	
Survey		1,000		
Loan	466	3,415	520	
Principle		3,000		
Interest	466	415	520	
Reserve		5,000		
Other	8,031		1,852	
Other benev.				$ 14,580
Subtotal, this page	$ 15,629	$ 19,415	$ 12,282	$ 13,489
Subtotal forwarded	114,594	108,971	114,993	14,580
Total	$130,223	$128,386	$127,275	$ 28,069
			Grand Total:	$155,344

The United Parish of Brookline
Preliminary 1972 Budget

Expense Categories

Salaries:	$87,865	Maintenance:		$20,322
Ministers	$44,475	Service	22	
Interns, music	3,900	Fuel, utilities	10,180	
Organists	4,170	Snow	250	
Choir	5,510	Organ	500	
Secretarial	15,970	Major	1,500	
Custodial	11,886	Insurance	7,870	

Housekeepers	754			
Teachers	1,200	Other:		4,580
		Printing	1,535	
Benevolences:		31,071	Office equip.	1,725	
Baptist	4,155	Audit	200	
St. Mark's	5,656	Interest	520	
UCC	7,975	Gifts, etc.	600	
UP pool	12,235			
Special off.	1,050	Subtotal		24,902
		Brought fwd.		130,442
Materials:		6,006		
Education	1,150	TOTAL		$155,344
Service	96			
Postage	1,400			
Office	250			
Janitorial	2,100			
Paper	250			
Music	80			
Books, periodicals	300			
Worship	380			
Programs:		5,500		
Education	1,700			
Advertising	2,300			
Communications	500			
Convention	450			
Young adults	400			
Meetings	150			
Subtotal	$130,442			

EXHIBIT 2
The United Parish of Brookline

Course Description for Cambridge Center for Adult Education Catalog, Winter, 1972.

Homosexuality—Robert Gallaway, Ph.D.
Clinical Psychology, Homophile Community Health Service—

These seminars will explore a variety of topics relevant to homosexuality, human sexuality, homosexuality and psychiatry, adolescent homosexuality, lesbianism and sexism, treatment and counseling, "gay" subculture, and law and public policy. Readings, case materials, and guest lecturers will complement class discussions. Limited to 20. 10 one-hour meetings. $22. Mondays, 4:15 P.M. Begins January 3.

EXHIBIT 3
The United Parish of Brookline
Provisions for use of premises in United Parish buildings

Bylaws of the United Parish 1970 (page 8)

Boards, committees, ministers and sponsored activities of the Parish or the individual churches shall be given preferential consideration in the assignment of the use of church real property for pursuance of their respective responsibilities where scheduling permits. Responsibility for assigning the use of church real property to boards, committees, ministers and others may be delegated by the Board of Business Affairs to an administrator or executive secretary (if there be one) in situations when it is impossible for the Board or the Council to act, the final responsibility shall rest with the minister currently serving as coordinating minister. That the Board of Business Affairs be empowered to approve placing in United Parish buildings any activity in which Boards and groups of the United Parish have a deeply vested interest and all other groups make application to the Council for use of any building.

April 5, 1970. The United Parish Council considered the idea that use of the buildings by outside groups for purely social meetings might not be the wisest choice (see vote concerning Daughters of Scotia). Consideration must be given to the amount of extra burdens on our custodial staff.)

The United Parish Council and Board of Business Affairs shall pass on all questions concerned with use of facilities in the United Parish *with certain exceptions:*—such uses without charges

Standard and Recurrent Uses

1. Religious meetings of the United Parish, participating (Baptist, St. Mark's, Harvard) churches and/or with other churches.
2. Business meetings of the United Parish and participating (Baptist, St. Mark's, Harvard) churches.
3. Meetings of church school, boards, and Committees of the United Parish and participating (Baptist, St. Mark's, Harvard) churches and any other authorized groups within the United Parish.
4. Meetings of denominational conferences, if schedules permit. (Some uses may be granted without fee or contributions. Some groups may wish to assist in costs involved at discretion of Board of Business Affairs.)
5. Use of parish facilities by members for weddings, receptions, funerals,

and similar services may be given without charge except that gratuities may be given to ministers or custodians in recognition of services.

General Regulations

Requests for use of facilities by any group—church-related or nonchurch-related, shall be made far enough in advance to the executive secretary—

1. To insure adequate consideration of the granting of permission.
2. Entry in the calendar to avoid conflict.
3. To allow adequate preparation for desired use.

Fees

1. Willett Hall (or comparable area)

Voting	$100 each occasion
Dramatic	$100 each occasion (includes preparation and production)
Others	$50 each occasion
	$75 each occasion with kitchen
	(including dishwashing by authorized person at hourly rate)
	Dishwashing must be included—groups must not wash dishes.

2. Parlor $25
   $30 with kitchenette (including dishwashing by authorized person at hourly rate)
3. Guild Room $20 (with parlor—see above)
4. Sanctuary $100
5. Chapel $35

Custodians	$15 each occasion
	$2 hourly rate dishwashing
Custodians	Schedule to be adjusted if necessary—should be done outside regular working hours (refer questions to chairman, Board of Business Affairs).
Organist	$15 Chapel—no rehearsal
	$25 Sanctuary with rehearsal

Board of Business Affairs should review procedures from time to time.

The executive secretary shall be responsible for materials, equipment, or clothing of groups using its facilities. Each group should provide safeguards for its members. This information must be given to all groups concerned.

Use of Organ: Policy approved by Music Committee of the United Parish (based on vote of Prudential Committee, Harvard Church, March 10, 1969)

The use of organ shall be restricted to the organist or someone approved by him.

Note: It is understood that with all new groups not parish-related, someone other than a member of the group must open and close the building. Arrangements to be made by the Board of Business Affairs.

EXHIBIT 4
The United Parish of Brookline
Current Requests for Space, Fall, 1971

Name of Group	When Here	Charge
Alanon (2 groups)	Tuesdays 7:30 P.M.	?
	Wednesdays 9:00 A.M.	?
Boy Scouts	Tuesdays 7:30 P.M.	no charge
Brookline Woman's Club		
Executive Board	1st Wednesday	$5.00 per
(11 times)	10:00 A.M.—12:00 m.	meeting ($55)
General Meetings	Twice a month	$30 per
(14 meetings)	Oct.-May, usually	meeting ($420)
	Monday 1-4 P.M.	
Deaconess Aid	1st Tuesday	church-related
	each month 11:30 A.M.	no charge
	2:30 P.M. (Nov.-June)	
Florence Crittenton Circle	Six times a year	$5.00 per
Unwed Mothers	on Wednesdays	meeting ($30)
	1-4 P.M.	
Headstart	5 days weekly	$100 per month
	Sept.-June	($850)
	8:30 AM.–1:00 P.M.	
Homophile Society		no charge
Counseling (individual)	Mondays 2-5 P.M.	
Group counseling	Monday evenings	
BHS—Black Respect Day	Nov. 23, 1971	church-related
		no charge
Parents Without Partners	Dec. 12, 1971	$50?
		$15—custodian
Brookline Mental Health Club	Dec. 17, 1971	no charge
Tau Beta Beta	Jan. 11, 1972	$50—pd.
Youth Group, Lunenburg	Jan. 15, 1972	no charge
	Jan. 23, 1972	
Drug Seminar—Boy Scouts	Jan. 16, 1972	no charge

Appendix (A)

The Practice of Homosexuality
and the Ethics of the Holy Scriptures

On February 11, 1971, the Lutheran Campus Council at Arizona State University in Tempe, passed the following motion: "Move that the Lutheran Campus Center accept the Gay Liberation proposal to utilize the center facilities one night a week as an opportunity for people to interact in an integrated human manner." The vote was 5 for, 2 against, and 2 abstaining.

Since that time the "gay libs" (homosexuals) have operated a gay lib coffee house on Wednesday evenings using the facilities of the Lutheran campus center from about 7 P.M. to midnight. I have stopped in at the gay lib coffee house a number of times. From what I have observed, there is no attempt made to present any spiritual orientation, but simply a social gathering place for homosexuals, both men and women, and a place to spread their doctrine that the practice of homosexuality is good and should not only be condoned but encouraged. Their literature was there in full display for anyone to pick up and read. I have several copies of their mimeographed newsletter, *The Arizona Gay Rap*, issues 1 and 2. Both contain want ads for Gay Crash Pads Needed. Here is a quotation from one of these want ads: "Accommodations will be made to fit your personal needs, such as 'men only,' 'women only,' 'don't call after nine,' 'gay preferred,' or whatever."

Directly beneath this want ad the following notice appears: "BULLETIN—Due to the shortage of condoms in the Valley, many are turning to Glad Rap." (Note: "glad" is another term for "gay" or "homosexual.")

Some of us through the years have been concerned over the permissive nature of the activities of our Lutheran Campus ministry in our center at A.S.U., but we have been constrained to be tolerant and understanding, realizing that we are living in an age of crisis and change when everything that is taking place today cannot simply be labeled black or white. But there comes a time when a limit has been reached, when permissiveness toward questionable practices can no longer be tolerated if a person is to maintain his integrity toward himself and his God. I believe we have come to that place and that time.

By providing a social gathering place for homosexuals, we of the church are not only condoning the practice of homosexuality but encouraging and promoting it. There is much fuzzy thinking being demonstrated about this matter that parades itself as wisdom and even as gospel truth. It is high time that we examine the practice of homosexuality in the light of the ethics of Holy Scripture.

I begin with an assumption, namely, that we still hold fast to the Scriptures as our final court of appeal. Our synodical constitution clearly states the doctrine of our church: "This synod acknowledges the Holy Scriptures as the norm for the faith and life of the Church." I ask you then to look at the practice of homosexuality in the light of *New Testament ethics*.

Please note that I speak here of *the practice of homosexuality* rather than of homosexuals. There is a difference. Here we must not be guilty of fuzzy thinking. Whenever we speak of the sinfulness of the practice of homosexuality, we are accused of "rejecting" a fellow human being, of sitting in self-righteous judgment of one whose emotional make-up may differ from ours. Nothing could be further from the truth.

Let us try to clarify our thinking right at this point. God is the author of all sexuality. He has placed sexuality within us. Therefore, sexuality *per se* cannot be evil, whether it be heterosexuality or homosexuality. This, I believe, is what the recent L.C.A. document on "Sex, Marriage, and the Family" tried to say, although it did not make the position crystal clear. It was trying to say this when it stated that a homosexual was a sinner in the same way as a heterosexual, namely in the abuse or wrong use of his sexuality. If the heterosexual indulges in rape, incest, adultery, or the like, he is sinful in the eyes of God because of the *malpractice* of his sexuality.

God's judgment of the *malpractice of homosexuality* is clearly stated in the first chapter of the book of Romans. Here it is, in the words of the Phillips' translation. The text speaks of the righteousness of God and the sinfulness of man.

Now the holy anger of God is disclosed from Heaven against the godlessness and evil of those men who render truth dumb and inoperative by their wickedness (1:18).

They gave up God, and therefore God gave them up—to be the playthings of their own foul desires in dishonoring their own bodies. These men deliberately forfeited the Truth of God and accepted a lie, paying homage and giving service to the creature instead of the Creator, who alone is worthy to be worshiped forever and ever, Amen. God therefore handed them over to disgraceful passions. Their women exchanged the normal practices of sexual intercourse for something which is abnormal and unnatural. Similarly the men, turning from natural intercourse with women were swept into lustful passions for one another. Men with men performed these shameful horrors, receiving, of course, in their own personalities the consequences of sexual perversity (1:24-27).

Continuing in the same chapter, "Moreover, since they considered themselves too high and mighty to acknowledge God, he allowed them to become the slaves of their degenerate minds, and to perform unmentionable deeds" (vs. 28).

Continuing at verse 32, "More than this—being aware of God's pronouncement that all who do these things deserve to die, they not only continued their own practices, but did not hesitate to give their thorough approval to others who did the same."

Those who defend their action in approving the use of the facilities of the Lutheran Student Center at A.S.U. love to repeat the words Jesus spoke to the woman in adultery after he saved her from death by stoning, "Neither do I condemn thee." But evidently they fail to hear His final admonition to this fallen woman now restored by God's forgiveness, or else fail to understand its implication, "Go and sin no more." The Lord did not water down the sinfulness of sin. He called her malpractice of her sexuality by the name that belonged to it, *"sin"*! Then he called her to a life of purity and self-discipline. "Go and sin no more."

Are we of the Lutheran Service Center saying this to those who "malpractice" their homosexuality? I have seen no evidence of this at the Student Center. For all practical purposes we are saying, "Come and continue practicing your homosexuality. Go and keep on sinning."

If we conducted a Christian counseling service for homosexuals (and also for heterosexuals whose perverse sexual behavior has separated them from God), we would be declaring in no uncertain terms to sinful human beings, "Go and sin no more." This would be approaching all of life from the redemptive viewpoint. It has been our hope and prayer that this would be the spirit of our ministry at the Lutheran Campus Center.

The Christian ethic is not one of permissiveness and licentiousness but one of self-control and discipline. The words "discipline" and "discipleship" have a common source. There can be no discipleship without self-discipline.

There is abroad in the Lutheran Church in the United States a spirit of extreme permissiveness. Any word of self-discipline and conformity to God's moral law is ridiculed as contrary to the Christian gospel. Absolutes in the moral realm are to such a person obsolete and fatuous. "We believe in a God of love. Don't speak to us of moral imperatives." What is this but a rebirth of the "antinomian" spirit, a heresy that has plagued the Christian Church from the very advent of the Gospel? The early church fathers fought it. Romans 6:1, 2: "What shall we say to them? Are we to continue in sin that grace may abound? By no means! How can we who died to sin still live in it?"

Luther fought some of his most valiant battles against the antinomians of his day. The battle continues in our day. Brethren, let us not become trapped in this ancient heresy.

The world is calling and crying for moral leadership in this confused day. If we of the church cannot supply it, who will? Quoting the One who died for us, "You are the salt of the earth; but if the salt has lost its taste, how shall its saltiness be restored? It is no longer good for anything except to be thrown out and trodden under foot by men." O Lord, have mercy upon us!

By continuing to condone and support the program now being conducted by the Gay Liberation Front in the Lutheran Service Center on Wednesday nights, I fear that we are placing the validity of our church in jeopardy in the light of God's Holy Word. How shall we escape the wrath of God's condemnation if we continue this course?

Brethren, my prayer is that you will consider this matter prayerfully and in all Christian charity.

Soli Deo Gloria.

Pastor

Chapter 5

Westbridge Village Congregational Church

prepared by M. B. Handspicker

Bill Roberts sat on one of the wire-spool tables in the coffeehouse and considered his alternatives. He was chairperson of the Board of Deacons of Westbridge Village Congregational Church, and the deacons sponsored the coffeehouse. It was the first night of the second year of its operation, and he held in his hand a letter from the chairperson of the Prudential Committee, laying down the terms of operation of the coffeehouse and stating in unequivocal terms the right of the Prudential Committee to decide whether it could stay open or not.

Westbridge

Westbridge was a large suburban community near New Haven, Connecticut. It had a fine school system, and many business and professional people, as well as university faculty, chose to live there. A sprawling community, it had three centers which the townspeople called "villages." When asked where they lived, Westbridgers usually answered, "the Village," or "the Heights," rather than simply "Westbridge." Once predominantly Protestant, since the thirties the Jewish population had increased to about 40 percent of the total, and since World War II the Roman Catholic population had increased as well.

The villages in Westbridge varied in character. Westbridge Plains had housing developments, built since the second World War, and was predominantly affluent and Jewish in population. The newer of the two high schools was located there, as well as an experimental middle school. Students from Westbridge Heights also attended these schools, although the Heights was mainly working class in population, and its people attended either the Roman Catholic Church or one of two small Protestant churches. Westbridge Village, which abutted the Heights, was considered by its inhabitants to be the coziest of the villages in Westbridge. It had a small square with a post office, numerous shops, an ice-cream parlor and delicatessen, and the Westbridge Village Congregational Church. Across the street from the church was a small playground which served as a gathering place for many of the youth from the Village and the Heights.

Adults from the Village were disturbed by what they considered the "goings-on" at the playground. Souped-up cars and motorcycles stopped by the playground, often blocking traffic, especially in late afternoon and early evening. On weekends the activity increased, and knots of teen-agers and young adults were there almost constantly. At one point, the local police, suspicious that there might be drug traffic in the playground, stationed an officer in the church tower to watch for such activity.

Westbridge Village Congregational Church

The Congregational Church was a fixture in the Village. Its lawn served as the village green, and commuters checked their watches by the tower clock. Founded in 1870, the church had reached its most prosperous years in the late forties, with large attendances and substantial budgets. In recent years its membership and budget had gone down, as had the percent of Protestant population. Members of the Village Church felt, however, that their church still had a mission in the community. In recent years they had sponsored a school for retarded children which met in church quarters, a Golden Age Club attended by many from within and without the city, and had formed an ecumenical Christian education program with the Methodist Church in the Heights.

Patrick Lowry, the pastor of Westbridge Village Church, had been heard to say, "We're a pretty warm community here. The members are friendly and open to new people when they come, although membership is not as large as it used to be." He cited the church suppers, the spring fair, and the carnival for elementary school children as evidence of the close community experienced by the members, and yet open to others. He felt that this was a pretty good record for a church whose membership was heavily weighted in the over-fifty bracket. "We are overjoyed when anyone under fifty shows up," he had once exclaimed. There were, however, sufficient members with school-age children that small but active youth groups continued for middle and senior high students.

The Seminarians

In the fall of 1970 two seminarians from Yale Divinity School, Don Ryder and Nate Reed, came to see Pastor Lowry. They were interested in setting up a Friday evening coffeehouse for high school kids, and after looking over Westbridge, thought that the Village was a good place to locate one. Pastor Lowry expressed interest, especially because he had not yet hired a youth worker for the year. But he asked, "Why do you think we need one, and why here?"

Nate said, "There's little for kids to do in town, especially here where there are no movies or bowling alleys. They just hang around the playground. And from talking with them we know there are drug problems, family problems, and drinking problems."

Don added, "We see the coffeehouse as an entree with the kids. We hope we can do some counseling with them as well as provide entertainment."

Pastor Lowry responded, "Your idea sounds great to me. Look, we haven't much money, but maybe we can develop a package that's worthwhile if one of you agrees to lead our youth groups too." They agreed to meet in a week and talk things over.

Assembling the Package

Pat Lowry first called Bill Roberts, the chairperson of the Board of Deacons. Bill, a schoolteacher from a nearby community, immediately liked the idea and offered to see if the deacons would agree to sponsor the coffeehouse. He called members of the board, and they all agreed that it would be consistent with the church's history of community service. Having received a positive response from Bill, Pat Lowry then sounded out the youth group. They expressed keen interest, and the president invited Don and Nate to come for an interview. Finally, Pat called Jack Nichols, a member of the Methodist Church and director of the Westbridge Community Center. Jack was sure that the center could provide thirty-five dollars a week to pay the seminarians for Friday evenings.

The next week the seminarians met with Pastor Lowry, the youth group, and Bill Roberts. After they had left, the youth group voted to request that they be hired as advisors. Next day Pat called Don and Nate, and they got together to make final arrangements. Don would advise the two youth groups, and help Nate out on Fridays; Nate would direct the program at the coffeehouse and help Don out when needed. They would split the money from the recreation department and the church.

The Coffeehouse

Don and Nate contacted a few of their friends at Yale who were interested in different kinds of youth work, and two or three volunteered to help out on Friday evenings just for the fun of it. They also got in touch with some of the local teen-age bands the church kids had told them about and began to book them for Friday evenings. They contacted John Lyman, chairperson of the Prudential Committee of the church, and received permission to use a storage room next to the parish hall for the coffeehouse "furniture." The furniture they had acquired by borrowing a truck from Donald James, the church moderator, and hauling in old wire-spools from the telephone company to use as tables. The last Friday evening in October they opened shop, and thirty or forty kids, including ten from the church, showed up. The kids felt the band was fairly good, the coffee adequate, and said they'd be back. By December the coffeehouse had eighty to one hundred kids showing up, a good many from Westbridge Heights as well as the Village, with some from other parts of the city as well.

The development was not without problems, however. There were sporadic arguments, some developing into fights. Usually the seminarians were able to keep things from getting out of control, and if they were not, the policeman on duty in the Village was always nearby. The main problem seemed to the seminarians to come from a slightly older crowd, mainly of young men; they hung around the fringes of the group and a twenty-year-old, named Gino Valenti, seemed to be their ringleader. They were in and out all evening. Some problems also developed with drunkenness; so they stationed one person at the door to check all drinks coming in—ostensibly from the ice-cream parlor across the street. On the whole, Don and Nate felt, they had had a pretty constructive fall. Kids were coming; some had responded to counsel; and members of the youth group were involved in community service.

Church Interest

From time to time during the fall, Bill Roberts was asked, "How is the seminarians' coffeehouse coming?" Bill and other deacons dropped in from time to time to chat with the youth group staffing the coffeehouse and with the seminarians. Bill responded to such queries with, "They're doing fine."

The Riot

By February Don and Nate felt they really had a good operation underway. The large attendance held up; there was less of a problem with drinking; they had seen only a little evidence of drug use. The third Friday in February seemed no different from any other coffeehouse night. But just at 11:00 P.M., closing time, Don and Nate and three of their friends from Yale were set upon by Gino Valenti and four of his sidekicks. The five seminarians were given a thorough beating. In the melee Don was able to get to a telephone and call the police. No sooner had they arrived than Mac Douglas, one of the deacons who ran a towing service, appeared in the doorway with a tire iron in his hand, shouting, "Where are the bastards?!" (He had heard the police call on his tow truck radio.) By this time the assaulters had disappeared, but the seminarians knew Gino and one other, and the police identified the others from descriptions the seminarians gave them.

Mac called Bill Roberts, and Bill arrived in time to talk with all the seminarians except one who had been taken to Yale–New Haven hospital for examination. He had concern for the seminarians, and also—as chairperson of the deacons—for the problems this posed for the coffeehouse project.

The Aftermath

In retrospect, the seminarians felt they should have known what was coming. They had suspected that Gino and his friends had been supplying liquor, and perhaps drugs, to the kids in both the Heights and the Village. They felt that they had put a dent in the amount of business the group was doing, and they thought now that their beating was probably the price they paid.

Feelings in the church crystallized. One deaconess asserted, "They can't close down *our* coffeehouse." Adults generally felt that their suspicions about the crowd in the playground had been accurate. When the trial of Gino and his friends took place, many members of the church attended; they felt the local judge had been too lenient in the past—passing out suspended sentences and probation to these same young men. Their hopes were realized when three of the young men were sent to prison, including Gino Valenti.

Some changes took place in the coffeehouse arrangements. Men of the church volunteered to come and just "be there"; a rota was developed and two adults were scheduled to be present each evening. Bill Roberts from the deacons, John Lyman from the Prudential Committee, and Hugh Koops, one of the younger deacons, were among those most often in attendance. The rest of the year went fairly smoothly, these men felt, and when the coffeehouse closed in the spring, just before finals at Yale, they looked forward to its reopening in the fall.

A New Year

John Lyman had been a regular attendant at the coffeehouse, and he had been disturbed by what appeared to him to be the sloppiness in discipline among the kids and their disregard for property. Once a door to the choir closet had been broken, and minor damage seemed to him to be endemic to the situation. When a new seminarian, Don Bornton, was hired in the fall of 1971, John decided that the Prudential Committee had better lay down some fairly clear guidelines about the conditions under which the coffeehouse could stay open (Exhibit 1). He felt that this was particularly necessary because Pat Lowry had resigned as pastor, effective the end of October, and John wished church leadership to be firm. He asked that Don initial the letter he sent and return it to him to signify his acceptance of the terms. John stressed in the letter, "Remember that permission of the Prudential Committee for the use of the parish hall for a coffeehouse depends upon your following the conditions set forth in this letter, and that the committee can review the situation at any time and withdraw its permission."

Don received the letter just before the first evening of the coffeehouse in October. That night Hugh Koops was one of the persons on duty at the coffeehouse, and Don showed him the letter. Hugh said to him, "Don't sign it until you check with Bill Roberts. The Board of Deacons sponsors this coffeehouse." Hugh called Bill, and he came down, read the letter, and wondered what to do. (For the responsibilities and powers of the relevant church committees, see Exhibit 2.)

EXHIBIT 1

To: Don Bornton
From: John Lyman for the Prudential Committee
Re: Coffeehouse for 1971-72 School Year
Cc: Bill Roberts, Board of Deacons

Dear Don,

The Prudential Committee is pleased to report to you that it has authorized you to run a coffeehouse in the parish hall, beginning the third Friday of October. This permission is given, however, under the following conditions:

1. Each Friday night there must be three male adults, at least one of whom must be a member of our church, who will be on duty in the parish hall during coffeehouse hours. One shall be stationed in the area of the choir robe closet and lavatories, one near the telephone and hallway to the dining room, and the third at the entrance from the street into the parish hall. They will help control the young people in their various areas and help insure that those entering are not under the influence of alcohol or drugs. They will be responsible for seeing to it that all exits are properly lighted and unobstructed at all times.

2. By the fifth meeting of the coffeehouse a notice will be sent to the general public, to the parents of the young people participating in the coffeehouse (whenever possible), and to church members outlining the purposes of the coffeehouse, its rules and regulations, and most important the fact that the young people who come are likely to be in and out of the building during the evening and that when they are outside there is no way to supervise their activities.

3. By the third meeting of the coffeehouse we will have a duplicated set of rules of behavior for distribution to those attending the coffeehouse, and this shall include rules on drinking, drug usage, gambling, necking in public, protection of church property, and provisions for the safety of everyone in the church. You must report any damage to church property, inside or outside, either prior to, during, or after coffeehouse meeting to the chairperson or vice-chairperson of the Prudential Committee. The same is true of any physical injury to any persons during those times.

Remember that permission of the Prudential Committee for the use of the parish hall for a coffeehouse depends upon your following the conditions set forth in this letter, and that the committee can review the situation at any time and withdraw its permission.

I hope that you will recognize that we do not mean to place a restriction on the activities of the coffeehouse. Our whole purpose is to insure the safety of both adults and young people involved in the coffeehouse activities, and to protect church property.

Please initial a carbon copy of this letter and return it to me to signify that you understand and agree to the conditions it sets forth.

(signed) John Lyman

EXHIBIT 2
Excerpts from the By-laws of the Westbridge Village Congregational Church

Article IV, Section 5: DEACONS

Deacons shall assist in serving the Lord's Supper, take in charge and distribute the parish relief fund, aid the pastor generally in his work, and provide a supply for the pulpit during its vacancy or in the absence of the pastor. At the first meeting of the board, following the annual meeting of the church, the board shall elect the chairman for the ensuing year. There shall be nine deacons. They shall hold office for three years, three being elected each year.

Westbridge Village Church

Article IV, Section 8: PRUDENTIAL COMMITTEE

The Prudential Committee shall consist of nine members elected at the annual meeting. The committee shall elect one of its members as chairman and one as vice-chairman. The committee shall have the following powers and duties: (a) to have the care of the property of the church; provide for its insurance; contract for its supplies and repairs; approve all bills and keep permanent records of all its transactions on file; (b) to consider the financial needs and program of the church as a whole; to draw up a budget for the current expenses and benevolences of the church; to present this budget to a Church Council meeting prior to the annual meeting of the church; to recommend to the church at its annual meeting the proposed budget with any revision that may seem necessary; (c) to act as a ways and means committee to raise the sums of money called for in the budget.

The Prudential Committee shall confer with the Church Committee as to any change in policy for the use of church property.

Article V: CHURCH COUNCIL

The Church Council shall consist of the pastor, two members of the Board of Deacons, two members of the Board of Deaconesses, chairpersons of all standing committees and a representative from each church organization. The moderator shall serve as chairperson.

The aim of the council shall be to coordinate the various activities and interests of the church, and to assist in their progress and development, with counsel and advice. All officers, committees and organizations represented in the council shall report regularly to the council.

Meetings shall be held three or more times a year at times to be determined at the planning session of the Church Council in June each year. Special meetings may be called at the request of the moderator, pastor, or any three members of the council.

Article VI, Section 2: CHURCH COMMITTEE

The Church Committee shall consist of the pastor, who shall act as chairperson, the Deacons, three Deaconesses selected by the Board of Deaconesses, the Superintendent of the church school, and the clerk. The duties of this committee shall be to act upon candidates for admission to the church, to consider cases of discipline, and to recommend to the church action on any specific question with regard to spiritual affairs which may arise. Meetings shall be held at the call of the pastor or of any two members of the committee.

Part II
The Church: Its Ministry

Chapter 1
Lil and Henry

prepared by Mac N. Turnage

A

Henry had become "deeply dissatisfied" with his program of graduate study and was considering giving it up to pursue a career in the ministry. But he did not want to interrupt Lil's work, which, for the first time, was interesting and important to her.

Lil sensed that Henry's studies were disappointing; but she avoided thinking about his misery. She had a job that was challenging for the first time in their six years of marriage-and-school.

They both wondered what steps they should take next.

School Career

For the past twelve months Lil and Henry had been "getting resettled both in location and in plans." In September 1971, he had begun the final year of his studies at Knox Seminary. Both of them had been eager to get through with his school career and to get settled into a parish. They had spent the time from June 1970 through August 1971 in Memphis, where Henry served an internship as student assistant pastor in St. Stephen's Presbyterian Church, a prosperous and successful church in a residential section. They both enjoyed the time there, and the experience made them eager to complete the final year of seminary and to get into a parish on their own. In college, Henry had majored in psychology and had used that training in his counseling at Memphis.

Lil and Henry were married at the close of their sophomore year in college, and their plans called for her to continue to work until he completed his training for the ministry. She secured a series of routine clerical jobs that she considered dreary—but a sacrifice she was willing to make. By being the breadwinner for a few years, she felt she was investing in their lifetime of work. She felt she was making Henry's ministry possible by working to support them until he finished his preparation for "their career." After two years of college and four years of seminary (including the internship), they anticipated the time when, as Henry had often said, "We will have our own nest and children, and a parish and a community where we can carry on our ministry."

However, during the fall of 1971, as he moved back into the academic disciplines, with the internship as practical background experience, Henry became aware of "inner urgings to teach." This interest was confirmed by conversations with classmates and friends on the faculty who could easily foresee a teaching career for him. However, on the one hand, knowing Lil's desire to get settled, to have a home, and to start their family, Henry was reluctant to redirect their lives toward graduate school. On the other, he felt that if he did not begin to get his credentials for teaching in the form of a graduate degree, it would be impossible for him to take these steps later. "It is now or never," he told her.

Lil confessed disappointment at the change of plans, but she decided that she could tolerate another year as a career girl while Henry did his master's degree. She was willing to postpone the family plans and to find "another humdrum job for another year."

Therefore, as his classmates interviewed churches which were looking for pastors, Henry prepared applications for graduate study in sociology and theology. He could continue at Knox, doing advanced study in theology or Bible; but he wanted to get away from the area where they had always lived, where they had done their college and seminary work, and where they were thoroughly established. New worlds were calling. He wanted to move into new territory geographically and intellectually. He was hoping to combine study of sociology and theology, to explore the church as a sociological force and church education as a process of socialization. He liked the program at Provincetown, where he could work in sociology at the university while getting his advanced degree in theology from the divinity school.

Graduate School

In the fall, Lil and Henry moved to Provincetown, and Lil found another dreary job. After working at it two weeks, however, she located a much more interesting and challenging position and began to settle in for the year.

At the time of registration, Henry discovered that the professor with whom he had expected to work was on an emergency health leave of indefinite duration. For a variety of reasons, other professors in Henry's field of interest were not teaching that term. He enrolled in a makeshift substitute for the program he had anticipated.

Within a month, Henry was wondering whether he should disengage from graduate school and move immediately into a parish. "Perhaps," he thought, "I made a mistake in pursuing this course, but I don't usually make this kind of mistake in understanding my own desires. At this point I can see no connection between the courses I am taking and the sense of vocation that brought me here. There is no longer the pull toward a teaching career as my form of ministry. Am I wanting to get into a pastorate because I don't like what I'm doing now? Pretty poor reasons for making a drastic change of plans —particularly when Lil is really enjoying her work, and that's an important part of our life here. At the same time, I've met several graduates of the divinity school here who are still hoping to get jobs as pastors, so I might be smart to stay on until the season when churches look to the seminary in their search for pastors." Half afraid that he was not able to adjust to new surroundings, he wondered whether he was leaving because he could not stand to live away from North Carolina or Tennessee, the area where he "knew God lived."

Lil was aware of Henry's discomfort, but she was also preoccupied with her delight in her new job. She enjoyed the people, and the work itself was interesting. She really felt that she was doing something worthwhile, that the job deserved her best efforts. She felt that this time she was learning—not hitchhiking on Henry's growth. "And after all," she told Henry, "it'll only be a year until we get settled in a place of our own. It promises to be a good year on the route. I can see that I will have to keep your morale up, while you continue your work on this degree, and that's a nice change. You don't have to boost my morale now."

Lil and Henry

B

Convinced that he was being guided to move out to practice the ministry for which he was trained, and apologetic that the change was uprooting Lil again, Henry announced his decision to withdraw from school. He wanted to be a pastor, not a graduate student or a professor. Their excursion into graduate study was ended.

Henry read Lil's reaction as surprise and disappointment. "No," she told him, "I'm not surprised. I know you've been miserable, and I knew that we would have to do something about it. I'm disappointed that we'll have to relocate again so soon, and I don't like to see you feeling that you've failed to carry through on an important decision. But I hope we won't have too long a delay in getting settled; I may be pregnant."

The Search Begins

Following his decision to leave, uncertain when a suitable call would come, Henry officially withdrew from school and went to work as an outdoor painter. Through official and unofficial denominational channels and through the usual personal contacts, he announced that he would like to be called to a pastorate.

As they waited for contacts to develop, Lil and Henry tried to clarify their preferences about the kind of work he should do.

The section of the country did not matter, they decided, but their connections were with the South. Both of them preferred a city, suburb, or town rather than a rural area. They analyzed themselves as the kind of people who like to have a lot of things going on around them, "even if we don't want to be noisily involved in all of them."

Lil was convinced that Henry should not get into a secondary role in a team ministry. She told him, "I know how hard you work. You have a good head, and you need a chance to use your training. Besides, I don't want to be the 'second wife'—the wife of the second minister." Her negative attitude about an associateship was major for Lil; Henry saw this factor as minor in their decision. A petite twenty-six-year-old, Lil still looked like a teen-ager. A friend had once told her, "You will still look like a fifteen-year-old when you are thirty-five." Henry was taller than she; but his beard did not make him look much older. On several occasions during his internship, people had asked, "Who is the little girl with our young minister?" For their self-respect and for the impact of their work, they wanted to move into the world with full adult status. They felt they needed to get away from the kid image.

Logan, Florida

The first opportunity they heard about was a parish in northern Florida. An elder from that congregation, Mrs. Martin, was visiting her son near Provincetown. Lil and Henry were invited to dinner and heard her describe her hometown, Logan, and the church there. The Presbyterian Church membership of about 125 was a cross-section of the town's white population of 3,500, and it included a large number of the community leaders. They had an open, frank conversation about the community, the congregation, and about Lil and Henry's future. However, after Mrs. Martin returned to Logan, they heard nothing more from her or the parish.

Pleasant Springs, North Carolina

In October, shortly after Lil's pregnancy was confirmed, the pulpit nominating committee of the Presbyterian Church in Pleasant Springs, North Carolina, their home state, invited Lil and Henry for a visit. From their investigations through presbytery officials and through Knox Seminary, the Pleasant

Springs group was interested in Henry as a candidate for their vacant pulpit. From the first, Lil and Henry indicated honestly that the rural scene was not their preference. During the visit, they saw the "separation from civilization" as a bother, but Lil and Henry both liked the people and the mountain scenery. As they left for Provincetown, the committee members asked them to give the position serious consideration.

Lil and Henry's conversations about Pleasant Springs centered around the problem of isolation, although they could identify several attractive features about Pleasant Springs. The people were the main appeal. The folks were obviously eager to have pastoral leadership; the church was no longer linked with a nearby congregation in a two-church field. In fact, the Pleasant Springs congregation had made commitments to increase their giving, so that they could pay the salary of a full-time pastor. The church had younger leadership than Henry had expected to find in a rural parish; but the hopes and goals of these leaders—beyond having a pastor of their own—were vague. They said they wanted to have a lively church and that they wanted it to grow. Henry had difficulty figuring out whether they expected the pastor to make it grow by his efforts or whether they were willing to take on new responsibilities. But they did seem to be open to leadership, vaguely willing to work, and cordial to him and Lil personally. Henry commented, "It is a fine rural parish and someone will have a good ministry there. The question is whether I am the one or not."

Lil was fond of the people; she liked the home for the pastor; and she sensed that the people liked both of them. She felt that all she could do there was raise children, but she was "willing to adjust to just sitting."

As they talked and prayed about this prospect, they tried listing positive and negative features, but they found that a single item in one column could outweigh several items in the other. "If a nominating committee were thinking about me 'yes' one day and 'no' the next, I would not want them to call me," Henry told Lil. Together they put an end to the process by deciding that "the Power at work in this process is not producing any firmness that we can identify with the label 'divine call.' " They had difficulty expressing their conclusion when they made the telephone call to say, "No, thanks."

Specialized Ministries

During the interval following this contact, Henry read lists of positions open in specialized and experimental ministries.

One urban church wanted a fresh graduate to help mobilize the congregation's resources for ministry in its immediate neighborhood. The description called for a minister to encourage the power structure of the community (many of whom were members of the congregation) to work for low-cost housing —through civic groups and organizations as well as through the church structures.

Another church, in the suburbs where large apartment buildings were going up, wanted a young pastor to serve on its staff and to develop a ministry to apartment-dwellers. The program was to be funded by denominational boards along with the local church and the presbytery, and the pilot project was scheduled for a two-year trial.

A third possibility sounded interesting to them; the church was located in a small town near a large city; a prestigious church-sponsored college was located there. The job called for a minister to bring together the college students and the disadvantaged of the community, using the manpower of the campus and church to expand the impact of the ministry.

All the job descriptions had appeal to them, but neither Lil nor Henry was excited about any one in particular. Henry summarized, "What I need is a chance to work at the basics of ministry, preaching Sunday to Sunday, for instance. And we both want to be involved in the total life of a total congregation, not in the fringe special features. I need to practice the fundamentals and to have the full pressure on me as the pastor."

Brandon, Virginia

In November, 1971, the next contact came from Frank Horton, Pastor of the Brandon Presbyterian Church in Brandon, Virginia. In his late thirties, Frank was recognized as a leader in the community, and carried heavy organizational respon-

sibilities for Presbyterianism in Virginia. His associate pastor
had resigned in September to take a position as a full-time
counselor in Charlotte, North Carolina. As associate in Brandon, he had carried major responsibility for the Christian education program; he and Frank had successfully built a team
ministry; they shared preaching and counseling responsibilities on a framework comfortable for both of them. Frank
supervised all the administrative work, but the associate had
worked in limited areas of general programming, too. Al-
together, it had been a happy relationship, and Frank was eager
to get competent help and to have the stimulating companion-
ship of another young clergyman. Theirs was the only Presbyterian church in the county. Located near the mountains, the
officials in the town of twenty-five thousand were busy with
efforts to bring new industry to the area.

Lil was not interested in Brandon; but she agreed to go with
Henry for the exploratory visit. She did not want to "dictate the
decision," but she said she could not "pretend enthusiasm,"
with Henry or with the Brandon people. Henry said, "I am
willing to look carefully at this possibility," but he described
his interest as "only mild."

As they analyzed the situation in Brandon, the dynamics of
the church relied heavily on Frank's personal gifts and on the
set of ties which he had built up in his six years there. The
senior pastor was expected to be a member of the country club,
and most of the leaders in the church moved in that circle.
Although Frank talked about "participatory church life," Henry
sensed that few persons in the congregation were strong
enough to take initiatives without clearing with Frank.

Church members pointed proudly at the program of ministry
to the community which they were developing. Scouts and a
daycare center were using church facilities. The Community
Action Committee was exploring the feasibility of several other
major projects, among which they would have to choose. Frank
and other pastors in town worked closely with the chaplain at
the state mental hospital nearby, and the chaplain was working
for credentials to offer training in pastoral counseling. From the
way their host and hostess "unloaded some of their personal

concerns and problems," Henry knew that there was no scarcity of work in the area of counseling.

Frank also described his hope for an "open, free-wheeling team to share responsibilities throughout the operation," but Henry suspected that subconsciously he would see himself —and others would see him—as an apprentice. "Working with Frank would do me or any other neophyte pastor good, but I've already done that bit."

When they talked about money with Frank and other church leaders, Lil and Henry were disappointed that the housing allowance would only cover the cost of rent for a small apartment.

As the pair were departing for Provincetown, Frank encouraged them, "Give me a call about any questions you want answered. The nominating committee will be meeting within twenty-four hours, and either the chairman or I will contact you as soon as the committee takes official action. But you know what the outcome will be, and we want you to move here and to work with us."

Before Frank called, Henry commented, "I do not want to spend every evening in committee meetings at the church, wherever we go." He observed to Lil, "All of our questions were being answered, but did you feel that we were being heard?" She answered with a quiet, pleased, "No, I didn't."

The next evening, Frank called, enthusiastic that the committee wanted to nominate Henry for the congregation's election as the new associate pastor. He also stated that he personally wanted Henry to accept. When Henry indicated that he and Lil were not really interested, Frank insisted that they think it over seriously for several days before giving a firm response.

Lil and Henry wondered what they would have to say when the week ended.

Lil and Henry

C

After reviewing their information and impressions carefully, after a full week's conversations, Lil and Henry had no regrets in saying no to Frank and to Brandon—except the uncertainty about what was coming next.

Lil's pregnancy was comfortable; she was in good health, and she continued to enjoy her work. Henry's work as a painter faded, a victim of winter weather. He grew restless about their prospects and about the process in which he was engaged.

He philosophized with Lil about their series of contacts with churches: "Everyone is busy proving 'I'm okay'—both the candidate and the church. It takes a lot of time and a lot of energy to get past this stage and to begin to communicate on a personal basis. What's needed is to build healthy human relationships; it's like dating and courting and engagement and marriage. Both parties need to be able to describe themselves honestly, with suitable encouragement-to-honesty flowing both ways. It's hard to build relationships when everyone's busy proving his own worth, and at the same time setting up arrangements to live and work together. I lean heavily on my conviction that, despite the awkwardness involved, God is dealing with all of us personally through this process. But I wish we could rush it up a bit."

As they reviewed the situation further, they found few results to show for the months of wrestling with the process. "Maybe we publicized ourselves too discreetly or too aggressively." Henry suggested to Lil, "We've looked at a lot of theoretical options, and we've turned down two firm offers,

Pleasant Springs and Brandon. And I guess we've made some discoveries about ourselves. At least, we've looked as much at who we are, what we want, how we want to live, what kind of work we're equipped to do—as much at that as we have at the job possibilities. I find it a valuable but uncomfortable era. Mainly, I wish we were making plans we could rely on."

Logan, Florida

Shortly before Christmas, Jack Smart, chairman of the pulpit nominating committee in Logan, called to invite Lil and Henry for a weekend visit. Henry was to preach; they were to have firsthand exposure to the possibilities there; and they would be under inspection by the congregation. Although Smart could not hide his discomfort with the process, he stated that the committee could not make any commitments beyond the arrangements for a visit. "But we like what we've heard about you from other people, including Mrs. Martin. And we don't know any other way to get acquainted with you except for you and your wife to come on down here for a weekend."

Henry assured him that he and Lil were interested in what they had heard about Logan and that they would not want to make any commitments until they could see the town and meet some of the people. He assured Smart that they appreciated having the whole set of arrangements and questions out in the open. Smart sounded relieved. A date in January, 1972 was set; arrangements were worked out in an exchange of letters.

With his wife Laura, Jack Smart drove the seventy miles to meet Lil and Henry when they flew to Jacksonville. Originally from Miami, Jack and Laura had decided that he would start his law practice in Logan with the idea that he would someday move into state politics. He liked the town, and he said that he liked the respect his fifteen years there had brought him. "I expect to practice law here the rest of my life," he said. "I want my kids to have a hometown; they won't have to cope with the problems of city life until they're old enough to choose to take on those problems. Someday I might like to be a judge; but I'm happy as a small town lawyer."

By the time they reached Logan, Lil and Henry felt that they had been given the chamber-of-commerce treatment, a homespun sociological analysis, and a warm welcome. The population was 90 percent white (mostly Protestant-preference), 10 percent black. As the county seat, it served the outlying agricultural area with shopping and services. Several small industries strengthened the economy. The schools had been quietly integrated, with "reasonable success," Jack reported. The White Citizens Council in the county "never got the upper hand."

Jack continued, "Oh, we go to the city for a 'big spree' now and then; Laura teaches piano part-time, so she makes me go to the opera; we're football fans, so we take in a couple of big games a year. But for the most part—politically and economically—we're middle America located in north Florida. How about you two? Are you liberals?"

The question threw Henry at first, but he regained his composure soon enough to state that he was a Democrat and that he considered himself a liberal person with conservative theology. He went on to say that he expected his ministry to focus on people rather than on public causes; but that he would expect to be free to speak out and act on social issues that concern Christians, or ought to concern them, today. He noticed that Jack nodded a gentle agreement, so Henry continued, "I'm convinced that the church, the organization, and the people, need to use their resources to help the community improve the lives of people. I hope to find a church where—with the people—we can figure how to go about this job." Henry could not, with confidence, interpret Jack's silent reaction.

The trip to Logan gave Lil and Henry some of the clues they wanted about the town and the church, and these clues were confirmed by their contacts with people in the church on Sunday. The church membership of eighty-seven appeared to be a fair cross-section of the community. Lil made it a point to meet two "blue-collar types" who showed up, and members of the congregation were proud to introduce a Mexican-American family who had settled there instead of continuing their migrant life. The Gonzales family appeared "awkwardly at home" with people in the church who told about having helped them through some difficult times.

As their host drove Lil and Henry around town, he pointed out the new hospital that served a three-county area, the low-cost housing being built, the new library, and the new courthouse. He stated that the town had received a state agency's award as "an outstanding municipality." Henry sensed that, although Logan was quite a distance from urban centers, it could not be considered a backwater. He noticed that members of the town council, the county board of education, and the hospital board were members of the congregation.

During the visit in Logan, Lil and Henry also talked with Mrs. Martin, who revealed that, following her conversation with them in Provincetown, she returned home and found that the nominating committee was involved in negotiations with another prospective pastor. This report explained the long silence that had followed their initial contact with her and —through her—with Logan. She did not state whether the candidate refused the overtures of the committee or whether the committee had lost interest in him.

When Lil and Henry met for informal discussion with the committee and other key leaders, the conversation flowed easily. They admired the older pastor who had retired a year earlier and had moved back to his family's farm in Tennessee. They talked about needing to improve the educational program in the church, and someone said, "We really ought to be doing something in the way of service, but we're not sure what to do and we don't know how to get started."

After their return from Logan, Lil told Henry, "I believe that my alone times could be happy times there. The town is small enough that I could get out on my own and get acquainted with people. I don't want to make the mistake of depending too heavily on you. The yard is big enough for children and a dog and maybe a garden. I like the people, but their conservatism scares me. I wonder how pious they expect us to be."

Henry mused, "It's not a city by a long shot, but the folks seem to be open. Like Pleasant Springs, they don't clarify what they want the leader to do, but they are not satisfied now. The salary is barely adequate, as I estimate the costs of living there." As he and Lil discussed the prospects, he asked, "What about the high school kids? They couldn't say much when we asked them what they would like to do in the church. In fact, they could not say much about anything. Will they relax with us later if we go there?"

They talked about the "plain vanilla" flavor of the town and the church. They confronted their disappointment that "no bells are ringing in us. We haven't had any overpowering visions, but we feel good about the prospect in general." They talked about Lil's role as the minister's wife and about "the gears I will have to shift in moving from my present job to a new kind of career; but I will have that problem wherever we go." They were still working at a blend, their understanding of vocation on the one hand, and the concrete realities before and behind them on the other hand, when Jack Smart called to report that the nominating committee and the officers of the church in Logan were ready to call a congregational meeting if Henry would consent to have his name presented. Jack said, "I hope you can give us an answer in a few days, and we hope that your answer will be as enthusiastic as our invitation."

Chapter 2
Chris Ripley

prepared by Richard Harmer

A

Chris Ripley was stunned. "That's unbelievable," he said. "That's absolutely unbelievable. It can't be true."

"Apparently it is," replied Ralph Linden, minister of the St. Andrew's Church, to which Ripley had recently come as curate. (St. Andrew's was located in Clifton, a suburb of a large metropolis.) "Mrs. Anderson—she's the director of Christian education over at the Union Church—discovered him herself . . . with her own son, Stewart, in the basement of their church."

Mr. Linden had just told Chris Ripley that the Reverend Roger Warner, the junior minister of the neighboring Union Church of Clifton, had been involved homosexually with a seventeen-year-old youth in his parish. "There was really no way for Roger to deny it, and I doubt that he would have. He also admitted to having an extensive physical relationship with the boy the previous weekend on our joint Labor Day outing."

"But that was six weeks ago," said Ripley. "Why have you waited until now to tell me about this?"

"I found out about it myself just two weeks ago," Mr. Linden answered. "Roger claimed it was a mistake. He said he was sorry it happened, that that was the only time it had happened, and that it would never happen again. He wanted the incident kept quiet, and he wanted to stay on in the parish. So, at least until he decided what he was going to do about the situation,

Frank Johnson (the senior minister at Union) was going to say nothing about it to anyone."

"However, Mrs. Anderson cried on several shoulders about the situation—and one of them was Mrs. Hammond's, our vestry council clerk," Mr. Linden explained. "When Frank Johnson heard from Mrs. Anderson that she had told Mrs. Hammond, he decided it would be better that I hear it from him than from Mrs. Hammond. So he came and told me about it. But he asked that I not tell you. He simply wanted as few people to know about it as possible until he decided what to do."

Linden continued. "That didn't work. Finally, I had to tell you. You're the one who deals most with Roger in our joint youth programs. Our kids are essentially your responsibility; and I felt you had to know. So Mr. Johnson agreed to let me tell you."

"But it's been six weeks now—has anything been done about it?" asked Ripley.

"In what way do you mean?" Linden asked.

"Well, they can't just sit on it and hope the whole situation will be forgotten," Chris Ripley answered. "They'll either have to deal with it openly in the parish, or Roger will have to leave."

"But Roger doesn't want either of those things," said Linden. "He wants it kept quiet, and he wants to stay. He says he wants to make his a redeeming ministry."

"But keeping it quiet and acting like nothing has happened can't work. It simply can't," replied Chris. "What has Johnson been doing about this?"

"Not much really, except agonizing. He's in a bind, and he hasn't figured yet how to get out of it. Roger wants him to act like nothing has happened. Against that stands the risk that it will eventually get out and the mess that would involve. He wants to be fair to Roger. Perhaps that's why he's taken so long . . . plus the fact that Johnson has been at Union Church for twenty-three years, that he's close to retirement, that he's been looking for an heir apparent, and that Roger was probably going to be that person. You know, Roger is his fifth junior minister in ten years. I understand one of the others had to leave because of a homosexual situation; and two left because of some other sort of problem. This may be beginning to reflect on Johnson's ability to pick a junior minister to succeed him."

"Well, what are we supposed to do while Johnson makes up his mind?" asked Chris.

"If something like that had happened here, with you, I'd have had to report it directly to the bishop," replied Linden. "He would have sent you off to a retreat for a week and would have had the thing thoroughly investigated while you were gone. By the end of the week, a decision on the matter would have been made. Whatever that decision would be, it would have been out of my hands once I reported it to the bishop.

"That seems not to be the case with their denomination," he continued. "Apparently, the decision is Johnson's. And he's having a hard time making it. I guess it's been a difficult time for the three of them. Mrs. Anderson's office stands between Johnson's and Warner's; and it seems that, since the incident, they've been having as little to do with one another as possible. There have been times they simply would not talk to one another."

"At least that explains why they've been postponing our joint staff meetings the last six weeks," said Chris.

"Yes, it probably does."

For the past two years, since Mr. Linden had come to St. Andrew's, the parish staffs of the two churches had met together every other week to discuss matters of mutual concern and to make plans for joint activities between the churches. The two churches had had a long history of good relations, and in recent years had combined many of their youth programs. In the last year, four other local churches had joined with them in a variety of ecumenical youth activities.

It was at the first of his joint staff meetings in early September that Chris Ripley had met Roger Warner. Roger had been in the ministry ten years, was thirty-five and married, with one son, and had come to the Union Church of Clifton the previous February. The two had struck up an immediate friendship. To Chris, Roger was a warm and open person—one of the most charismatic people he had ever met. Many members of both parishes had responded to Roger in the same way. Chris had been very pleased that he and Roger would be working closely together as leaders of the two churches' youth programs.

Chris asked Mr. Linden again what he thought they should do about the Warner situation. "There's not much we can do," replied Linden. "I'd like to help them get this thing resolved. But it is their church; and no one from our parish has been involved directly.

"I am concerned about our young people, though," Linden continued. "What would we have done if that boy had been from our parish instead of theirs? That kind of involvement with our young people is still possible, because right now we're going along as if nothing had happened; and Roger is still spending nearly every night with the kids from all six of the churches in one activity or another. I've heard his wife is complaining all over town that she's so lonely, and Roger is never at home with her. I guess until this thing gets resolved one way or the other, we're just going to have to keep close tabs on him to make sure it doesn't happen again."

"And because I'm the one that works closest with him, I guess that job falls to me, doesn't it?" Chris Ripley replied.

"I guess it does," responded Linden.

"Does any of the other clergy in the ecumenical group know about Roger's situation?" Chris asked.

"No," Linden answered, "at least Johnson doesn't think they do. Right now, he wants to keep it that way. So you're on your own, and I don't think it would be a good idea to tell Roger you know."

Three weeks later, Frank Johnson had still not brought the matter to a resolution. As far as Chris Ripley could tell, he had discussed it with no one in the Union Church. In the meantime, Chris found himself frequently dropping in on activities Roger was supervising. Eventually Chris felt he had to let Roger know that he knew of the situation.

"I suspected you'd been told," Roger replied. "It is pretty obvious when you're suddenly there, wherever I turn."

Roger continued. "You're all making much more of this thing than you should. It was a mistake—an accident. It will never happen again. I was fooled. I thought Stewart was just getting very attached to me. His father pretty much ignores him. I didn't realize what he had in mind; and he got me in a situation I couldn't get out of. Believe me, I'll never let anything like that happen again. Never."

Chris didn't know whether to believe Roger's version of the story or Mrs. Anderson's. Mrs. Anderson claimed that Warner had seduced her son. Stewart apparently didn't want to talk about the affair with anyone; and Mrs. Anderson was not allowing anyone to try to talk to him about it.

"Whatever the case is," Chris replied, "you've got to deal with the situation. You can't let it get beyond your control. If you're willing to sit down and talk about it publicly with your parish—tell them you've had this problem, this is what has happened, you want them in your parish to know about it, you want to stay with them, and ask for their help—if you'll do that, I'll sit there alongside you and support you. If you're not willing to do that, then leave this place quietly and quickly. But, for God's sake, don't drag us all through the painful process that has to happen if you try to stay here and keep it quiet. Don't do that."

"But if I go to the parish with it," Roger answered, "I'll be branded a homosexual for the rest of my days in this town. And that's not true; I'm not. I want to stay here in Clifton; but I don't want that kind of yoke hanging around my neck."

"But something's got to be done," Chris said.

"I know," replied Roger. "And I wish Frank would make up his mind, whatever he's going to do. I feel trapped—like a caged animal. His indecision has me paralyzed. Why can't he make a decision, one way or another. Just let me know my fate."

"If I were in your position," volunteered Chris, "I think I'd turn to a friend that's 100 percent for me and talk it out with him. I can't be that friend, because I've got a vested interest in the outcome. But is there someone that could be 100 percent for you?"

"Yes," Roger replied, "but I couldn't stand to tell him."

"Have you gone to see a psychiatrist about this?" Chris asked.

"I went a couple of times," Roger replied, "but then I stopped. It was ridiculous. It wasn't going anywhere."

"Didn't Johnson insist that you continue?"

"No. He wasn't going to press it unless the psychiatrist could guarantee that I'd never get involved that way again. But that's not the point anyway. The point is that I'm not a homosexual. So there's no reason for me to go. If I went, it would be taken as an admission of guilt. Look, I'm married. I've got a son. Why can't any of you believe me?"

"I'm sorry, Roger," Chris replied. "Right now I just don't know what to believe."

Over the next two weeks, nothing had been done by Mr. Johnson to bring the situation to a resolution. When pressed by the St. Andrew's clergy, he had promised to "take care of it by next week"—but had consistently failed to do so. In the meantime, as Chris continued to appear at youth activities Roger was leading, relations between them deteriorated.

Chris had also become concerned about a sixteen-year-old youth from the St. Andrew's Church who seemed to be spending more and more time with Roger over at the Union Church.

Chris brought this matter up with Roger. "It seems you and Jerry Fredricks are spending a lot of time together."

"He's learning guitar," Roger replied. "He's not very good, and I'm willing to listen to him and give him some encouragement. That's more than his parents are willing to do."

"Right now," Chris said, "considering things as they are, I don't think it's a good idea for him to become too invested in you."

"That's ridiculous, Chris," Roger replied. "You're letting a wild imagination get the better of you. There's nothing going on between us. The kid's perfectly safe. You have absolutely nothing to worry about."

"Well, I don't approve of the relationship that's developing between you," Chris responded. "If you're not willing to terminate it yourself, I'm going to intervene actively and woo the kid away from you."

At that point Roger exploded: "OK, that's it. There will be no more spying on me. Either trust me or take your kids and get out. I've got nothing more to say about it."

During the next week, Mr. Johnson again failed to take any action. Chris Ripley began hearing reports that Roger was telling people that he was jealous of Roger's popularity with the young people and that he was trying to subvert him. Several parishioners had also come to Chris asking about rumors that something was amiss at the Union Church. He felt something had to be done soon.

Chris Ripley

B

In response to the situation described in the previous section, Mr. Ripley, in consultation with Mr. Linden, decided to sever formal relations with the Union Church at the youth level. They called a brief meeting of St. Andrew's five youth advisors and read them the following letter, of which separate copies had been prepared to be sent to young people in the St. Andrew's Parish and to their parents. The text of both copies read as follows:

Beginning this Sunday evening at 7 P.M., St. Andrew's Parish will offer alternative programs to the existing Sunday night joint youth programs and ecumenical youth activities at the Union Church. We can no longer continue to support these programs with staff commitment.

It is our reluctant conclusion that, given the vulnerability of adolescents, the two programs require more adequate supervision than is now available. By offering alternative programs at our own parish, with leadership accountable to us, we will be able to provide the necessary supervision.

> Yours truly,
> (signed) Ralph Linden, Rector
> Christopher Ripley, Curate

When the youth advisers asked for a further explanation from Messrs. Linden and Ripley, Ripley answered, "All I can say is that it has become very apparent that Roger Warner and I are not getting along, that trust has broken down between us. I can't say any more." At that point the meeting was ended.

The next morning the letters were sent out.

Chris Ripley

C

The letter touched off several months of turmoil and recrimination for both churches. Although some of their youth advisers accepted Linden's and Ripley's decision because it came from their ministers, others did not. The day after the letter was sent out, one of them called Roger Warner to get an explanation of what was going on. That evening, Warner met with a number of the youth advisers from the two churches, staying until 3 A.M., and told them the entire story of his involvement with the Anderson boy, including the explicit details of each sexual encounter he had had with the boy—identifying the boy by name. Warner also maintained that he was not a homosexual—that the boy had compromised him.

After that, everything exploded. The boy's father threatened to kill Warner. St. Andrew's vestry came down hard on Linden and Ripley for not having acted on their knowledge sooner. Others, who were sympathetic to Warner, criticized them for acting too hastily; and some, who believed Warner's denials, denounced Linden and Ripley for character assassination. Chris, in particular, became the object of a great deal of criticism from all sides for his "handling of the situation."

After the story of the incident had come out into the open, Warner's wife revealed to Ralph Johnson of the Union Church that a similar thing had happened at the church from which the Warners had previously come, and that it had been the reason for their leaving that church. Roger Warner's personal record, signed by the senior minister at his former church, had contained no word of the previous incident. However, when Mr. Johnson contacted that minister, he confirmed Mrs. Warner's story. When Roger was confronted with this information, he continued to deny that he had had any previous homosexual encounters.

It took the Union Church another two weeks after this disclosure before it asked for Warner's resignation, and another six weeks before they asked him to leave his house, which stood adjacent to the church. (By then his wife and son had left to stay with relatives.)

However, Warner did not leave town. Instead, he took a job at a local department store; so he could stay in town and maintain contact with the group of about fifteen people from both churches who continued to support him. At one point, there was some discussion among them about their starting up a new church.

During this period, Chris Ripley wrote to an organization on the East Coast that helped place "gay" ministers. However, Warner refused to have anything to do with them.

Six months after the incident became public, Chris moved to another suburb of the city. After he had left, he heard that Warner had for a time tried circulating within the "gay" community there, but had left it.

Nearly a year after the incident, while attending a homophile conference, Chris described extensively Warner's case to a psychiatrist, to the point of role-playing his behavior, including his vehement denials of homosexuality. The psychiatrist's diagnosis was that Warner's problem was not homosexuality *per se*; but rather, some psychopathological disturbance, of which his homosexual behavior was only one manifestation. He told Chris that, with the consent of a consulting psychiatrist, he would have had Warner committed.

Soon after talking with the psychiatrist, visiting briefly back in Clifton, Chris learned that Roger Warner had finally left to take up a new ministry he had found in a neighboring state. Nothing about the incident in Clifton had been passed on by Mr. Johnson in Warner's personal record when he had sent it to Warner's new ministry.

Chapter 3
Greg Wright and Twin Rivers Presbytery

prepared by Louis Weeks

A

Greg Wright ushered the case-writer into his office, full of old furniture, mimeograph equipment, and an eclectic library of theology and urban affairs. "Would you like some coffee? Black, sugar, cream, or both?" His own cup in hand, Wright launched directly into a recitation of the events that would culminate in the meeting of Twin Rivers Presbytery on the following Tuesday.

"It all started when a fellow right down the street, who belongs to the Communist party, asked me to talk to a friend of his who was coming through Metropolis on his way to New York. Sam, the guy from the neighborhood here, already knew I was not a Communist, and he certainly knew I didn't belong to the American Communist Party. Anyhow, I said I would talk to his friend.

"They wanted to get the American Communist Party on the ballot here in Missouri. They argued that once it was on the ballot, as it used to be before the McCarthy era, people might treat it more as a political party in the media and in considering its platform. I remember my reaction. "Why don't you ask party members? Why don't you ask other people who believe in freedom of speech and such? Why me?" They argued that I, as a minister, had freedom to act courageously; while most other people would be summarily dismissed from their jobs if they

Names and places have been disguised. This case was prepared as a basis for class discussion rather than an illustration of either effective or ineffective handling of an administrative situation.

signed as electors to get them legally on the ballot. I guess I was most impressed by the list of folk they had approached to sign, people who had refused for one reason or another. Their refusal to sign convinced me that the fear of communism is still very much alive and that steps must be taken to guarantee people's freedom of speech. People have to be able to associate without fear of job or social reprisals.

"I talked it over with Cindy, my wife, who is in law school here at the Metropolitan University, and we figured we should take the risk. We recognized that many people would not approve of this exercise of our constitutional rights, but we thought the election board would not publicize the people signing, and we also thought there was at least the possibility that it would do some good for the whole Left. So I signed.

"I really think somebody has to stick his neck out. Otherwise we never will move past the days of Joe McCarthy when red-baiting was a national sport. The fear of communism and the fear of being called communistic have been used repeatedly to destroy or damage movements for social change. Even Dr. King was vulnerable to this, and the false accusations that he was a Communist did cost him some support.

"Look around you here in the neighborhood. Right around us here it's black mostly. But the color is not the main thing. We all suffer, white and black. Every time we try to do anything, those people say, 'It's a communist plot.' When all we want is justice—just equality before the law.

"We're trying to get a civilian police review board established here in the city. Some people asked if my signing for the Communists wouldn't hurt that effort. Well, you've seen the papers. They were already accusing us of being Communists even before I signed. Maybe if people accept the American Communist Party as just another political expression, then red-baiting won't work any longer. I don't know for sure though; all I can do is hope.

"Anyhow, the papers did get hold of the lists in response to Right Wing letters, names of electors for all parties. Then on the floor of presbytery, Allen Stiles said he thought Twin Rivers Presbytery ought to investigate me. And the presbytery referred it to their Department of Ministerial Personnel. I met with the department, and I really thought the session was a constructive one. This is what they came up with, and I really agree with most of it." Wright reached in his desk and produced the following report.

Report to: The Presbytery of Twin Rivers
From: The Department of Ministerial Personnel
Ernest Billings, Chairman

Concern of This Report. At its Stated Meeting on Wednesday, May 10, 1972, held at Oak Grove Presbyterian Church, Twin Rivers Presbytery heard the concern of some of its members that the Reverend Greg Wright had been listed in the public press as being one of the electors for the Communist party. Mr. Wright read a statement indicating that he had been so listed and reporting that, whereas he had not been and was not now a Communist, he responded affirmatively to the request that his name be used in this way out of strong civil libertarian convictions. After brief discussion, the following motion was adopted by the presbytery, referring this matter to the Department of Ministerial Personnel:

> The Reverend Allen Stiles moved that the Department of Ministerial Personnel consult with the Reverend Greg Wright about his being linked with the Communist party as an elector for its slate of candidates and report its findings back to the presbytery.

Departmental Work with the Concern. As directed by the action of presbytery, the department met with Mr. Wright on Friday, June 2, 1972, for a conference from 3:00 to 4:30 P.M. Members of the department present were: Lawrence Dundee, Ellen Taylor, Ernest Billings, James Forest, Dwight McDonald. At the outset of the dialogue, Mr. Wright was asked to read the two statements which reflected his position in this matter. The first of these, printed below as statement 1, was prepared and signed by Mr. Wright and others several months ago when, on March 10, they filed as electors for the Communist party. The second, printed below as statement 2, was prepared by Mr. Wright when he learned that complaints and questions about his action were being heard by different ministers, and that this concern might reach the floor of presbytery.

> *Statement One:* We have consented to the use of our names as candidates for presidential and vice-presidential electors on nominating petitions of the Communist party in the 1972 general elections. While not necessarily members of the Communist party and not necessarily in agreement with its political principles, we

have consented to appear on its nominating petitions because we believe that it, as well as every other political party, has the democratic right to present its candidates for president and vice-president and because the electorate should be accorded the democratic right to choose, among every and all political parties, the candidates for whom they vote.

Statement Two: It has come to public attention that I am one of the electors for the Communist party in Missouri.

Attached is a statement which all the electors subscribed to some months ago, prior to the filing of the petition with the Secretary of Public Affairs.

I am not now, nor have I ever been a member of the Communist party. I am not fully in agreement with their principles, although I believe that certain of their ideas do have merit.

I agreed to be an elector basically because I am a civil libertarian, and I believe that *all* political points of view and parties have a right to be heard and debated in the marketplace of ideas, and to put forth candidates for public office. The right of the Communist party to organize and put forward its ideas has been abridged by law in the past, and continues to be limited because of an irrational fear of association with the term "communist." Some of this fear may be alleviated by virtue of the Communist party's appearance on the ballot and its recognition in law as a legitimate political party. America has been strengthened in the past by minor parties which have provided a means for people to vote no to the majority parties, and to put forward ideas which at a later time have been incorporated into the platforms of the major parties, and eventually into law.

Following the reading of these two statements, the conversation of the department with Mr. Wright centered primarily around three issues: (1) Whether he had considered the impairment of his own effectiveness in the decision to take this action. (2) Whether he had considered the burden that others in the presbytery would have to bear as a result of his action, such as extended complaints, reduced or canceled gifts, or even termination of memberships. And (3) how the presbytery might minister to the deep-seated and frequently irrational fears associated with communism, which still persist in our society and which produce strong negative reactions to an action like that of Mr. Wright.

The department did not question the *right* of Mr. Wright to permit his name to be listed as an elector. Neither on ecclesiastical nor civil grounds could an indictment be brought for that. The freedom of individual Christians, lay or professional, to hold diverse political philosophies, is well established. Thus, even *if* Mr. Wright had affirmed those dimensions of communist philosophy which may be compatible with the Christian faith, there would be no grounds for censure. As indicated in the three issues listed above, the concern of department was with the wisdom of his action and with the context of our culture which makes his action an issue in the first place.

Mr. Wright responded to the first issue by indicating that, yes, he had considered the impairment of his own effectiveness. The concern that different political perspectives be heard and represented in the election process was overriding. He was moved by the conviction that where such freedom is denied to some, it may soon be lost by others. Further, he felt that those open to understanding his rationale might come to respect his position even though continuing to differ with his judgment.

The second issue had also been considered, though Mr. Wright had hoped that the names of electors would not receive such public attention. Mr. Wright regretted the fact that one price we pay for membership in a connectional church is that the actions of some, even though taken as individual citizens, may place a burden on others. He reflected that persons ministering to minority groups at times bear the burden of actions of others in the denomination which reflect racist attitudes.

The third issue above was discussed briefly, but was judged to be beyond the mandate and functional responsibility of the department. The very fact that the action of Mr. Wright was referred to the department, however, points to the need for education in relation to communism. To say that the day when communism was considered "the enemy" seems to be passing, or to point to the growing dialogue between Christianity and communism, particularly in European countries, indicates that the time may now be ripe for deeper understandings.

Recommendations. In light of the above dialogue held by the department, the following recommendations are offered:
1. That this report be received and printed in the minutes;
2. That presbytery reaffirm the right of its members to hold differing political perspectives and to act on these as the individual conscience dictates; and
3. That presbytery direct the Department of Education to establish a task force to
   (a) Prepare an educational program for a meeting of Presbytery in the near future on the subject of communism; and
   (b) Develop resources which may be used by local church groups which may wish to study this issue.

Wright waited patiently for the case-writer to read the document. "I showed them some of the more obvious places where I disagreed with the stated platform of the party, in their attempt to legislate an end to racist or sexist remarks or propaganda, for instance. I'm against every attempt to constrain freedom of speech, and I would have to oppose these parts of the party's platform for the exact same reason that I am signing to have them represented on the ballot in Missouri."

"Did all the flack come from outside your congregation? From the presbytery and from the papers?" asked the case-writer.

"One man left. He told the session that it was on account of my signing, but for a long time his wife had been after him to join the Tenth and L St. Baptist Church. He had been on the verge for quite a while, and everyone knew it. No, mostly people have been open, and even those disagreeing have been supporting my right to do what I did. For us here at Good Shepherd, it's been educational. We've seen that it's just a step from red-baiting to repression for anybody. Black Americans know about oppression, and they know too about my reasons for seeking its end. Oscar Willard, who represented Good Shepherd at that first meeting of Twin Rivers, spoke beautifully of the need for freedom to speak and to assemble in the U.S.—how these rights were in danger. He said he knew me, that I was no Communist, and that critics should come see the work that the church is doing in housing and other areas of need.

"What happened after the department report appeared?" asked the case-writer.

"Well, I reckon you saw some of the letters (Exhibit 1). In addition, several ministers called to say they had gotten calls or conversations about the decision. People seemed to object most violently to the idea that the presbytery should study communism, although surely they wanted to see me punished too. (Possible avenues of disciplinary action are explained in Exhibit 2.)

"Ernest Billings called another meeting of the department. He evidently circulated a supplemental draft to replace the first one, and at the second meeting of the department they passed a supplemental report that corresponded almost exactly to the one he wanted. They did not invite me to that second meeting, and Billings called it when Jim Forest would be out of town. I don't honestly know if it was by coincidence or by design, but I had heard Forest led the thinking of the department for a study of the issues in the first meeting. At any rate, this is what they came up with." He showed the case-writer a second document:

Supplemental Statement to the Report to Presbytery
from the Department of Ministerial Personnel
Concerning the Reverend Greg Wright

Most ministers and ruling elders are aware that as a result of an action of the presbytery meeting of May 10, 1972, the Department of Ministerial Personnel was directed to meet with the Reverend Greg Wright to discuss the circumstances of the news article announcing his having signed the ballot of the Communist party of Missouri. This meeting was held on June 2, when all available members of said department met for two hours. The result of that meeting was a drafted statement mailed to all ministers and session clerks, along with copies of the statements given by Mr. Wright in the May presbytery meeting.

As a result of this statement there have been some letters, phone calls, and letters to the editor. If one could cite the main tenor of these calls, letters, and public communications; it is to the effect that Mr. Wright should be severely reprimanded and criticized by the presbytery. To use stronger language (some did), Mr. Wright should have been soundly disciplined and firmly dealt with. A second implication of these communications was that the presbytery, by its action through this department, indicated a condonance of Mr. Wright's actions.

The response we, as a department, make is that in the case of censure or ecclesiastical discipline, there are fairly clear, spelled-out guidelines in the *Book of Discipline*, and in our best judgment, no censure was applicable. Our department strongly advised Mr. Wright that many in the presbytery regretted his action and that he may have indicated poor judgment and a lack of sensitivity to and responsibility for his brothers in Christ and the church by his action. However, this department had no recourse, in its best wisdom, but to uphold and reiterate to the churches the principle of freedom of political decision on the part of all citizens, even if this action seems reprehensible or misguided or inappropriate to others. This department in no way condones Mr. Wright's actions, nor feels that anyone but Mr. Wright can be responsible for them. It has been suggested that this action on Mr. Wright's part was "disruptive to the peace, purity, and unity of the church" (a directive of the church discipline and our ordination vows as elders and teachers). However, it is incumbent on this department humbly to remind each of us to what degree we as critics are disruptive of the peace, purity, and unity of the church, as well as to remind Mr. Wright.

In the communications to the presbytery there were some alarming innuendoes to the effect that Communists are to be dealt with so severely and harshly as to be nonpeople. We again respectfully remind presbytery that—however vehemently we reject the ideology of those we disagree with, or repudiate their morality—as Christians, and particularly as church leaders, we are admonished by Christ himself to love our brothers, and even further, to love our enemies. Mr. Wright stated to the Presbytery and to our department that he is not, nor had he ever been, a member of the Communist party. Our department believes him, and for those who do not, we nevertheless plead a patient, Christian consideration and love.

Some have criticized the suggestion of our department that churches may want to elect to have a study and dialogue on communism. This suggestion was intended as a permissive recommendation and seems to us a rational alternative to the deep emotions toward communism in our society. The suggestion by some that we do not have to study that which we know is antithetical to Christ does not seem to us entirely adequate. There are deep emotional feelings related to many issues within our society. It seems a necessity to have knowledge about a wide spectrum of people in our society even if we disagree with them because of our personal faith in Christ.

In light of the criticisms mentioned above, the Department of Ministerial Personnel considered the issue again at its September 1, 1972, meeting and decided to provide this further clarification of its action.

Further, we felt that it would be helpful if our recommendations to presbytery make it clear that we do not condone Mr. Wright's action. Hence we have amended our recommendations to presbytery as follows:

1. That presbytery express its regret to its churches that the Reverend Greg Wright allowed his name to be used as an elector for the Communist party.

2. That presbytery reaffirm the right of its members to hold differing political perspectives and to act on these as the individual conscience dictates.

Let us reiterate the fact that these two amended recommendations replace the recommendations of the initial report and that these are the recommendations you will be asked to vote on at presbytery.

"The substance of that report," Wright explained, "will be to censure me without judicial process. It just completely capitulates to the radical right. This report is negative, and it makes me mad. I took the first one to be essentially neutral, which is the way a presbytery should be regarding the political actions of a member. And the recommendation to study the issues presented by communism sounded like the best part of it. That's what we should be doing—studying the issues that confront us.

"Now the second report talks about my considering the 'peace and unity' of the church. I do. But do the middle-class people who speak out or act in racist ways against the poor and the black consider that they disrupt the peace and unity of the church for us? Billings is worried about a loss in money and people as a result of my action. I told him that was the price of a membership in a connectional church. Just think of the effect on our evangelistic efforts when a white church refuses to get involved with a black one. Even when they dedicate a forty-thousand-dollar organ or a new building, while we brothers and sisters in Christ are trying to keep a family from getting evicted over a twenty-dollar utilities bill, don't you think that hurts us? We all pay a price for being together, but we try to insure one another's freedom in Presbyterian government. That's the freedom I'm asking in the political realm for the people just to accept the party like any other.

"Now we are trying to figure out what tack to take in the coming meeting of Twin Rivers Presbytery. There are all kinds of possibilities. On the one hand, other things are going on in the world and in my own ministry. I could back down from my stance, ask that my name be removed. Maybe I could just apologize, and that would be enough. I do believe in the importance of the civilian police review board; Metropolis needs one desperately. Our projects in establishing low-income housing for the poor and for seeking jobs in community businesses for blacks are worthwhile too. If signing for the party seemed to be getting in the way of those things, then I could remedy the situation by backing down. But colleagues in presbytery urge me not to go that route, and I'm not sure I could anyhow.

"On the other hand, I sincerely believe that Presbytery has no right to investigate or to act on the political beliefs of its members. Some people asked me if I would have done the same thing for the American party, American Nazis, or someone such as that. My answer has been that there seemed no shortage of people to sign for Right Wing things. I guess I could include some members of presbytery among the probable interested people. The American Civil Liberties Union did back rights of the American Nazis and of the Klan too. I support them. I guess you could say I might have signed for the same reason. Whatever political persuasions, however, presbytery is in where they have few rights if any. I could just refuse to go to the meeting, indicating by my absence that I consider them breaching their commitment to me. There again, though, friends might feel I am going it alone when we are all in this together.

"Between those poles lie a whole range of options. I could offer a substitute motion, for example, asking that the first set of recommendations be passed instead of the second. The first set of recommendations appealed to me. They indicated a constructive use by presbytery for making use of feelings provoked by my action.

"Then, too, I could just put the extenuating circumstances, the ambiguity in the second document that seems to condemn me without due process, and move for recommittal to the Department of Ministerial Personnel. I could try to amend the report, or to get seriatim consideration of it. There are lots of opportunities to make people stand and be counted.

"I do think the Presbyterian system works well in this situation, though, as it does in general. I would like to make the best of the moment for constructive change. How to go about it? That's the question."

Rising to go, the case-writer asked if there were any other things pertinent to the decision that should be included.

"Yes, I guess three things need to be said. The first is that it has not been without cost that I signed. I don't know exactly what the outcome will be, but I have been under fire from presbytery where I should be getting support for freedoms guaranteed under the constitutions of both church and state. But, second, and much more important, we are all in this together. If people don't have the freedom to speak out and do what conscience says without violating the rights of others, then the nation and indeed the whole world is deep in trouble. I am very much affected by both those things as I make my decision. Third, before presbytery meets, several of us will be getting together to try to work out a way to react. Would you like to come?"

EXHIBIT 1
(From *The Daily Globe*)

To the Editor,

According to a news article in the Daily Globe on June 3, a committee of Presbyterians will not recommend censure of the Reverend Greg Wright for allowing his name to be placed on the Communist party ballot.

Have these good Christians forgotten that some fifty thousand Americans died in Korea? And that the late Dwight Eisenhower's "peace with honor" abandoned about four hundred Americans to rot in Chinese Communist prison camps? Have they forgotten some fifty thousand Americans killed in Vietnam plus our POWs? Those Americans chose to fight and die on foreign soil rather than one day having to fight the Communist on American soil.

By force, the Communists have taken over twenty-nine nations, linking millions of people. Because we were the No. 1 power, they knew they could not defeat us militarily so they used a different approach. Infiltrate the government, universities, news media, and churches; promote issues such as war, poverty, racism to turn Americans against Americans; attack all anti-communist movements and organizations, calling them extremists and Facists.

On June 19, 1962, the late Nikita Krushchev predicted, in a speech in Bucharest, Rumania, that: "The United States will eventually fly the Communist Red Flag. . . . the American people will hoist it themselves."

Janet Willis
2201 Valley Road
Metropolis, Missouri

To the Editor:

Devout Christians should not be surprised at the recent announcement of a local church denomination that "the day when Communism was considered 'the enemy' seems to be passing. . . . The time may now be ripe for deeper understandings." Discerning Christians have long predicted that dreadful day when Satan would feel sufficiently secure to employ such a monstrous distortion of truth.

"Deeper understandings of what?" we ask. "Of a Communist party openly

*dedicated to the total enslavement of mankind?" Of a party that systemati-
cally imprisons, tortures, and kills literally thousands of Christians whose
only "crime" is a steadfast refusal to deny Jesus Christ?*

*We confess an inability to understand any minister or religious group that
shows such overweening concern for the so-called "Communist party" (actually a band of international gangsters). But we hang our heads in greater
shame and sorrow that nowhere has this religious group shown similar
concern for our brothers in Christ—members of the Lord's own body—who
even now suffer horrendous persecution at the hands of the very political
system this local denomination so passionately embraces.*

*Let all true believers, therefore, take warning! "Be well-balanced, temper-
ate, sober-minded; be vigilant and cautious at all times. Your adversary the
devil prowls around like a roaring lion, seeking someone to seize upon and
devour. Withstand him; be firm in faith—rooted, established, strong, immova-
ble and determined—knowing that the same [identical] sufferings are appointed to your brotherhood [the whole body of Christians] throughout the
world" (I Peter 5:8-9).*

*The Reverend Gilbert Haven
6702 Fleetwood, Metropolis*

EXHIBIT 2
*Excerpts from the Presbyterian Book of Order relating to
Greg Wright and Twin Rivers Presbytery*

Presbyterians are strongly committed (some would say preoccupied) with the
meaning and process of church government. Certain rights and duties are set
for congregations, for sessions, for presbyteries, and for general assemblies.
Those things not specifically mentioned are reserved to individual Christians.

From the Preliminary Principles:

31.01 1. That "God alone is lord of the conscience, and hath left it free from
the doctrines and commandments of men which are in any thing
contrary to his Word, or beside it, in matters of faith or worship."
Therefore they consider the rights of private judgment, in all matters that respect religion, as universal and unalienable: they do not
even wish to see any religious constitution aided by the civil power,
further than may be necessary for protection and security, and, at
the same time, be equal and common to all others.

31.03 3. That our blessed Savior, for the edification of the visible Church,
which is his body, hath appointed officers, not only to preach the
gospel and administer the sacraments, but also to exercise discip-

line, for the preservation both of truth and duty; and that it is incumbent upon these officers, and upon the whole Church, in whose name they act, to censure or cast out the erroneous and scandalous, observing, in all cases, the rules contained in the Word of God.

31.04 4. That truth is in order to goodness; and the great touchstone of truth, its tendency to promote holiness, according to our Savior's rule, "By their fruits ye shall know them." And that no opinion can be either more pernicious or more absurd than that which brings truth and falsehood upon a level, and represents it as of no consequence what a man's opinions are. On the contrary, they are persuaded that there is an inseparable connection between faith and practice, truth and duty. Otherwise it would be of no consequence either to discover truth or to embrace it.

31.07 7. That all church power, whether exercised by the body in general or in the way of representation by delegated authority, is only ministerial and declarative; that is to say, that the Holy Scriptures are the only rule of faith and manners; that no church judicatory ought to pretend to make laws to bind the conscience in virtue of their own authority; and that all their decisions should be founded upon the revealed will of God.

Of the Presbytery:

42.01 1. A PRESBYTERY consists of all the ministers, in number not fewer than twelve, and at least one ruling elder from each church, within a certain district which includes at least twelve churches. Every ruling elder duly elected to be the moderator or other officer, a chairman of a standing committee, or a member of the general council of a presbytery, may be enrolled as a member of the presbytery for the tenure of his office, but he need not be simultaneously a delegate from his church. In mission territories outside continental United States and in extremely isolated areas within continental United States upon recommendation of the synod of jurisdiction, the General Assembly may permit presbyteries to be organized with fewer than the minimum number of ministers and churches provided for above and with a quorum less than that provided for in Section 6 of this chapter, provided that there shall be at least five ministers in every presbytery and a quorum shall always include at least three ministers.

42.06 6. Any four ministers, and as many ruling elders as may be present belonging to the presbytery provided that at least two churches are represented by ruling elders, being met at the time and place appointed, shall be a quorum competent to proceed to business.

42.07 7. The presbytery has power to receive and decide appeals, complaints, and references brought before it in an orderly manner, and in cases in which the session cannot exercise its authority, shall have power to assume original jurisdiction, provided that cases may be transmitted to judicial commissions as provided in the *Book of Discipline;* to receive under its care candidates for the ministry and to dismiss them to other presbyteries; to examine and license candidates for the ministry;

Questions asked ministers on their ordination:

The moderator shall ask the candidate to answer the following questions:

49.04 1. Do you trust in Jesus Christ your Savior, acknowledge him Lord of the world and Head of the Church, and through him believe in one God, Father, Son, and Holy Spirit?

49.04 2. Do you accept the Scriptures of the Old and New Testaments to be, by the Holy Spirit, the unique and authoritative witness to Jesus Christ in the Church universal, and God's word to you?

49.04 3. Will you be instructed by the Confessions of our Church, and led by them as you lead the people of God?

49.04 4. Will you be a minister of the word in obedience to Jesus Christ, under the authority of Scripture, and continually guided by our Confessions?

49.04 5. Do you endorse our Church's government, and will you honor its discipline? Will you be a friend among your comrades in ministry, working with them, subject to the ordering of God's word and Spirit?

49.04 6. Will you govern the way you live, by following the Lord Jesus Christ, loving neighbors, and working for the reconciliation of the world?

49.04 7. Will you seek to serve the people with energy, intelligence, imagination, and love?

49.04 8. Will you be a faithful minister, proclaiming the Good News in word and sacrament, teaching faith, and caring for people? Will you be active in government and discipline, serving in courts of the Church, and in your ministry, will you try to show the love and justice of Jesus Christ?

49.04 9. When installation is held in connection with the service of ordination, continue with Form of Government, Chapter XX, Sections 13 and 14.

49.05 5. The candidate, having answered these questions in the affirmative, shall kneel for prayer and the laying on of hands by the presbytery.

Committee on Ministerial Relations:

57.01. A COMMITTEE on ministerial relations shall be established and elected in each presbytery in order that the spiritual and temporal welfare of the ministers and churches under its jurisdiction may be properly maintained.

57.03.   The committee on ministerial relations shall function in the presbytery in the following ways:

57.03 1.   a) Direct access to this committee shall be had at all times by all ministers in the presbytery, and by all ruling elders in the presbytery in active service, in all matters relative to the spiritual or temporal welfare of the churches in which severally they hold office.

57.03 2.   b) The committee on ministerial relations may visit and counsel with churches and ministers of the presbytery as to their spiritual and temporal welfare.

Of Discipline:

81.08.   Offense. An offense is anything in the doctrine, principles, or practice of a church member, officer, or judicatory, which is contrary to the Word of God or to those expositons of its teachings as to faith and practice which are contained in the Constitution of the United Presbyterian Church in the United States of America.

81.09.   Kinds of Cases. Every case in which there is a charge of an offense against a church member or officer shall be the subject of judicial discipline and shall be known, in its original and appellate stages, as a judicial case. Every other case shall be the subject of administrative discipline and shall be known in its original and appellate stages as a non-judicial or administrative case.

Of Jurisdiction:

82.01.   Original Jurisdiction. The several judicatories exercise original jurisdiction within their respective spheres, but when a lower judicatory neglects or is unable to exercise proper discipline in a particular administrative or judicial case, the higher judicatory shall assume jurisdiction in the case, and either issue specific instructions to the lower judicatory as to its disposition or conclude the matter itself. Original jurisdiction in its relation to ministers belongs to the presbytery; in relation to all other persons to the session.

Of Judicial Process:

83.01.   Definition. Judicial process is the orderly succession of legal proceedings, in accordance with those principles and rules which have been established by the Church for the conduct of a judicial case.

83.02.   Basis of Judicial Process. Judicial process against an alleged offender shall not be instituted unless some responsible person under the jurisdiction of a judicatory of the United Presbyterian Church in the United States of America undertakes to sustain the charge; or unless a judicatory finds it necessary for the purpose of judicial discipline to investigate the alleged offense. Such investigation shall be made by a special committee of investigation, elected by the judicatory. If the investigation indicates that charges should be made against the alleged offender, the special committee of investigation shall prepare the charges and specifications for presentation to the judicatory.

When an offense has been committed under such circumstances that it is impossible for the offender to be prosecuted to conviction, judicial process shall not be instituted until God in his righteous providence shall give further light.

Of Charges, Judgment, Censure:

84.01. Form of Charge. Every charge must be presented to the judicatory in writing, and must set forth the alleged offense with the specifications of the facts relied upon to sustain the charge. Each specification shall declare, as far as possible, the time, place, and circumstances of the commission of the alleged offense, and shall be accompanied with the names of the witnesses and the titles of the records and documents to be cited for its support.

87.01. Judgment Without Full Judicial Process. If a person commits an offense in the presence of the judicatory, or comes forward as his own accuser and makes known his offense, the judicatory may proceed to judgment without full judicial process, giving the offender an opportunity to be heard; and in the case first named he may demand a delay of at least ten days before judgment. The record must show the nature of the offense, as well as the judgment and the reasons therefor, and an appeal may be taken from the judgment, in which case the judicatory becomes an original party, and shall appoint one or more of its members, or other persons under its jurisdiction, to defend its action in the higher judicatory.

89.01. Degree of Church Censure. In judicial discipline there are five degrees of Church censure, namely, admonition, rebuke, suspension, deposition, and excommunication; and when any one of these censures shall apply, the judgment shall be pronounced by the moderator of the judicatory in the name and presence of the judicatory.

The Presbyterian minister has right of appeal to Synod, then to General Assembly, on several specified grounds and to her unspecified grounds determined applicable by the next judicatory.

Greg Wright

B

Before the time of the informal caucus of Greg Wright with several supporters, he received word that the Department of Ministerial Personnel would meet again. He was invited to participate in the meeting and speak in favor of either the first report or a substitute proposal in two parts offered by one member of the department for that meeting:

The proposal, an amalgam of the first two, read:

"1. That Twin Rivers Presbytery reaffirm the right of its members to hold differing political perspectives and to act on these as the individual conscience dictates.
"2. That the presbytery communicate to its churches that its action in the above recommendation is not in any way to be construed as supportive of the Communist party or suggesting its approval of the individual action of the Reverend Greg Wright, who permitted his name to be used as an elector of the Communist party in Missouri."

Since Wright had to leave the meeting before any votes were taken, he did not know what decision the department had made when the group of his supporters met informally before the presbytery meeting.

Wright, members of the caucus, and members of presbytery graciously allowed the case-writer to be present and to take notes both before and during the meetings which followed.

To the six members of presbytery gathered early with Wright, the minister explained how the department might offer a second substitute to the original recommendations. The caucus decided to try for an adoption of the initial report of the department, which had included the direction of presbytery's Department of Education to establish a task force, permitting programs and resource development for study of the subject of communism. They felt that this possibility not only would exonerate Wright but would help open the subject for study. Moreover, in the words of one pastor, "Some good might come of it all yet," if the study produced less paranoia in the churches.

That members of Twin Rivers Presbytery were nervous and excited about the matter was obvious from the first of the formal meeting, convened promptly at 9:00 A.M., Tuesday, September 19. The moderator made several allusions to his own feelings of anxiety, and anticipatory laughs accompanied each expression. After opening worship, and the formalities of recognizing visiting people, he introduced Ernest Billings to present the report from the Department of Ministerial Personnel.

Billings asked first that presbytery receive the texts of his reports, without any of the recommendations, as a preface to recommendations and an explanation to those who cared enough to read the minutes. His motion passed unanimously. He proceeded to read the department's recommendations, which were the two proposed for the third meeting. (see p. 145).

Billings asked that the recommendations be considered *seriatim*. He recounted the difficulties which the department had encountered in achieving consensus on these recommendations, and asked for prayerful debate and for mature voting.

Ed Waters, pastor of a small church on the outskirts of Metropolis, immediately asked to amend the second recommendation to include reference to Jesus Christ, stating, "I move to amend that second one to add 'and reaffirm our faith in Jesus Christ and the gospel as the savior of us all.' " His amendment failed for lack of a second.

An unidentified (to the presbytery) layman rose to state that "the problems here are simple ones. Can a person hold views that are anti-Christian and still be a minister? The two ideologies can't be together." He claimed that he did not call for Wright's censure, rather he wanted a simple statement of what ministers can and cannot do. "It's not a question like 'Can a person support George Wallace as a Christian?' " he concluded. "Rather it is, 'Can one be a Christian and also an anti-Christian?' "

The moderator asked future speakers please to identify themselves for the sake of those who did not know them.

Milton Walpole, a layman from the First Presbyterian of Metropolis, sought to amend the first recommendation to read: "That presbytery reaffirm the right of its members, *within the standards of discipline*, to hold differing political perspectives and to act on these as the individual conscience dictates." His amendment was passed after a lengthy discussion in which Walpole indicated he assumed the Department of Ministerial Personnel had determined no standards had been violated by Wright.

Further discussion of the main motion included statements by two laymen.

"I'm wanting to go home tonight and tell my wife and children," said one, "that Twin Rivers Presbytery will have nothing to do with communism." "I want to go to work tomorrow," he continued, "and tell folk there that our hands are clean of anti-Christian wrongdoing. I don't know exactly how to go about this. But that's what I feel."

"I travel all over Missouri," said the second, "and the reports I hear are all negative. I sure respect the right of a person to sign for something. But it's a case of bad evangelism. It doesn't have to be just bad evangelism in this day and time, my own daughter heard about dialing people at random and telling them God loves them. She spent all yesterday afternoon on the phone calling people with amazing results. That's good evangelism. Why can't we have good evangelism from Twin Rivers ministers?"

After discussion, however, the first recommendation passed by a substantial majority. Focus turned to the second, for which Bill Wheeling, pastor of Fourth Presbyterian, offered the following substitute: "That presbytery express its regret to its churches that the Reverend Greg Wright allowed his name to be used as an elector for the Communist party, and disapproves of such action."

Dr. Reich, who taught at a Presbyterian seminary near Metropolis, spoke against the substitute: "This language can only mean that Christianity and Marxism are by definition incompatible. This is not necessarily the case." He proceeded to outline some European attitudes embodied in the Marxist-Christian dialogue. "Even good Marxists recognize the limited horizons in the communist eschatology. And all good Christians must hail as constructive efforts to identify with the oppressed in society. After all, that is the way of Jesus himself, who said he had come to heal the sick, make the blind see, free the captive, and liberate the oppressed."

Dr. Reich concluded by declaring that presbytery had a right, perhaps even an obligation, to divorce itself from Wright's action as an individual, but in his opinion the substitute missed the whole point.

"If you professors would get your nose out of books and put your ear to the ground, you would see that communism and Christianity are polar opposites," responded an unidentified person from the floor.

James Forest, who had not spoken thus far, rose to explain that as a member of the Department of Ministerial Personnel, he considered the substitute as probable grounds for appeal to synod and General Assembly by Wright since it amounted to censure without due process.

Steven Yardlee, a prominent Metropolis lawyer, stood to take issue with Forest's interpretation of the substitute. "I don't see the technicalities of censure here at all. It just expresses an opinion." Several members of presbytery applauded Yardlee's words, and the moderator asked everyone to refrain from emotional response such as this.

The chair recognized Dr. Charles Gravely, Pastor of Metropolis' First Presbyterian Church and a well-respected member of long-standing in the presbytery. "Brothers, I worry that our meeting will lose its vitality and constructiveness if such outbursts continue. I hope we will be reminded of Mr. Billings' words of counsel, that we have prayerful debate and mature voting on this issue."

Gravely spoke forcefully in favor of the substitute. "We, as ministers, are linked with our public stances as a part of the connectional vows we take. I very much admire Mr. Wright's general attitudes and his Christian commitment to the Lord's service. On more than one occasion I have stood with him in unpopular causes. You know I respect his good motives—civil liberties are exceedingly important, often terribly inconsistent. Of course, we all make mistakes—and should not be afraid to admit them. As for the legality of the substitute, let's not be determining by little technicalities and fail to heed important things."

A good friend of Wright's, Josh Hasting, made a lengthy speech in behalf of the defeat of the substitute. He said that not only were there Christians who were Communists, particularly in Europe, but that even Jesus himself was much closer to sinners and prostitutes than to the people with all the money in his day. "If the Communists in our country are oppressed, then we have the duty to free them from oppression," he concluded. "I know Greg Wright, and I know he did not do this lightly. He was very much concerned to witness to people about his Lord and Savior, and this action was consistent with his ministry in seeking housing and help for the poor and needy of Metropolis. We should back him up."

After much further discussion Wright himself stated that according to the *Book of Order* admonition was censure, that he took the substitute for admonition and, therefore, would certainly appeal if it passed.

"I am reminded of the words of a German pastor under Hitler who said that he was silent when the Nazis came for the Jews, did not speak out when they came for Catholics, was silent when they came for labor leaders, and that by the time they came for pastors there was no one to speak out for him." Wright continued. "If the civil liberties of some of us are withheld, then the rights of us all are impaired and in jeopardy. I'm no Communist. You've seen me stand here and defend the right of all kinds of people to speak, even if they are wrong. Don't rebuke me for doing something to preserve the freedoms we all cherish."

Ed Wong, student pastor at Metropolitan University, and a

former North Korean refugee, declared that it was indeed a problem of civil liberties. "I lost some of my own family to communism," he said. "We ought to be careful to protect our freedoms, as Greg Wright is doing, even when it is not popular, or else there will be no difference between the Free West and communism. Moreover, we need, as people are doing in my own country, to seek ways to live together, or hate will keep us apart. The freedom to express opinions and take positions in politics lies at the very foundation of our best ideals."

Dwight McDonald, another ministerial member of the department, declared that he was inclined to vote for the substitute. "We keep trying not to step on anybody's toes," he argued; "but we don't need pious disclaimers. We need to recognize that as the presbytery grants freedom to its members, so it also requires discretion in exercising that freedom. We are just being forthright and clear. We are not exercising censure."

McDonald then proposed another substitute: ". . . And that the presbytery form a special committee to investigate possible grounds for censure of Mr. Wright." The moderator ruled this substitute out of order, since presbytery already had a substitute motion on the floor.

Lawrence Adams, who frequently spoke to Twin Rivers Presbytery on the need of supporting conservative causes, stated that he had no intention of harming Wright. "But," he confessed, "it is inconceivable to me that presbytery can't say, 'Mr. Wright, we oppose you in love and kindness, and we just don't like your judgment.' "

After Adams spoke, Lawrence Dundee called for the question, which was put and passed (80-48). The substitute lost (62-47). The recommendation carried (60-52).

Jim Forest proposed now that the original third recommendation of the department be undertaken, and he moved for a Department of Christian Education Task Force to be established "(a) to prepare an educational program for a meeting of presbytery in the near future on the subject of communism, and (b) to develop resources which may be used by local church groups which may wish to study this issue."

It was now getting close to lunchtime, and discussion for and against the motion was more abbreviated than the debate surrounding the first two recommendations. A pastor who had formerly served several congregations in Germany and in Lebanon, who now taught at the seminary, stated that one of the refreshing things in modern theology was the "theology of hope," grounded firmly in the Marxist-Christian dialogue. "We had better listen as well as speak to the Marxists," he said, "for people, particularly those in desperate conditions of starvation and hopelessness, are not so much interested in 'pie in the sky by and by.' What they want, in the words of Mohammed Ali, is 'the pound on the ground while they're around.' " He claimed that the people of God always have hesitated to confront what seemed alien. "They're not giants, they're just men," he said, "and we should teach them and learn from them."

On the other hand, a public school teacher claimed that "this is something that ought to be studied in social science classes, not in the churches." He declared that communism is a social-economic system, and it should be treated as such.

Two others spoke, one for and one against the recommendation arguing that the timing was not right. One said it was needed enough to continue, even though conflict was the price. The other said that the present controversy would really discolor any education on the subject. He said that if presbytery educational personnel did work through congregations willing to undertake study of communism, nothing would be objectionable. It was just that to formalize the study now would create the impression that Greg Wright was supported after all.

After the discussion, Twin Rivers Presbytery defeated the recommendation, (42-75). Presbytery executive, Bill Evans, called "the order of the day," since it was already past lunchtime. On the way to eat, Jim Forest approached Greg Wright: "I think we have the tacit authority to get going on some kind of informal study with willing churches. I wonder what we could do to inform them about communism and its dialogue with Christianity?"

PART III
The Church:
Community Issues

Chapter 1
Easter Sunrise

prepared by Louis Weeks

Since Gene and Ina Ross were winsome and interested, Bill Stovall asked them to become advisors for the Centerville Presbyterian Youth Group. He explained to them that junior and senior high students met together, and that Gene and Ina had freedom in the direction of youth activities. He set up a meeting with the young people themselves, at the Ross's request, for a discussion of their possible service as advisors. "I know they will be delighted," said Stovall, the superintendent of church school. "Several of the young people asked particularly for you if you were willing to come."

At the meeting, Gene and Ina presented some of their ideas: that young people should plan and direct their own programs both for worship and service; that young people should be vitally involved in all the work of the church; and that advisors should be resource people more than chaperones, police, or directors. The young people were asked about their own responses to the Rosses and to these ideas. Unanimously they expressed hope that the Rosses would undertake to advise them, that they would rely on the Rosses for resources and take charge of planning and supervision themselves, and that they really looked forward to the coming year. Gene and Ina took the job, enthusiastically.

The Rosses had not lived in Centerville very long—by small

Names and places have been disguised. This case was prepared as a basis for class discussion rather than an illustration of either effective or ineffective handling of an administrative situation.

town standards. Fifteen months before Gene had received an offer from Centerville Furniture to head their sales department. When they visited the town, they found that Joe Black, who served as president of the company, also chaired the school board. He assured Ina that she could be hired as a teacher, and asked her which grade she preferred. When she said "Anywhere from grade two to junior high, but I like fourth grade the best," Joe got on the phone and in a few minutes reported, "Hey, good news. They have a vacancy and need a fourth-grade teacher. Why don't you go and interview this afternoon?" By the following week, Gene and Ina were all "fixed up," according to Joe, who sent a school contract for Ina to sign along with a contract for the house they really liked (and at their price, almost). Giving proper notice in Warrentown and selling their house there meant that the Rosses moved seven weeks later. Some men from the company helped them get the house and yard in good condition, and scarcely two months from the time of the original offer, they were well situated in Centerville. "Boy, was that easy," said Gene to Joe, over lunch.

The Rosses found Centerville very much what they figured it would be—a typical small town, with a score of country-club families living on Moon Lake outside town, another dozen or so families of influence living closer to the business district, a number of small shopkeepers and middle production and sales people at Centerville Furniture, Kitchen Cabinets, Wonder Fibers, and Kiddy Clothes, the town's four plants. Most of the town's schoolteachers and leaders came from among these families. Almost all the workers in the factories, at the town's stores, and for nearby farms came from the remainder of the white population. A community of blacks lived on the edge of Centerville, mostly low-income people who served as domestics in the homes or nonskilled labor around town, and several of whom were unemployed. In the words of Joe Black, "any Negroes with get-up-and-go had got up and went" to Arlington, a larger city in a nearby county, where job and social opportunities were more abundant. Nevertheless, Joe proudly pointed to the facts that two of the long-tenured workers at

Centerville Furniture were black, that one newly hired teacher was also, and that the children of this neighborhood attended the Centerville schools "just like everyone else."

The Rosses also found life in Centerville to be about what they had expected, only a little bit friendlier. For the most part, they worked and lived quietly and developed several close friends. Aside from a few local eccentrics, everyone proved amiable and helpful to them. They received invitations immediately to several homes for dinner, to sail and to ski on Moon Lake, to attend cocktail parties, and to other goings-on. They were also invited to worship at several churches. In Warrentown they had belonged to a United Church congregation, and since there was none in Centerville they agreed to shop around. They visited Baptist, Methodist, and Lutheran churches in turn, but finally decided on the Presbyterian Church because many of their new friends belonged. Joe Black had been an elder there, and now served as a teacher of high school students in the church school. After joining, they grew to like the minister, William Jennings, not so much for his sermons (which were often pretty dull) as for his apparent depth and wisdom in dealing with troubled people. They became fast friends with the Stovalls, Martha and Bill, who also played bridge and liked similar things as the Rosses. And the Lowry family, too, Gene and Ina really enjoyed; Pete, Sallie, Ted, and Louise (stair-step children) soon called them "Uncle Gene" and "Aunt Ina."

Gene and Ina, in a word, found Centerville delightful. His work was not terribly taxing, yet it was challenging. Hers was sheer pleasure. Their one real disappointment was that they continued childless. Examinations and some medications had not helped. They talked of adopting children, but what with their full-time responsibilities and all, they decided against it. After all, she was teaching "the greatest group of children in the world," and he was helping with the Centerville sports program. The Lowry children acted like their own; and Sallie had stayed with them while the rest of the Lowrys vacationed in the mountains. Then along came Bill Stovall with the invitation to lead the youth group!

The Rosses embarked on the new "duties" with pleasure. They invited the youth group leaders over for pizza and discussion of the year's plans. Susan Renfroe, the president, said she really wanted them to do some serious Bible study. She also hoped they could go to a retreat in the mountains the following summer. Jim Tenney, the program chairman, said they needed to learn about other ways of worshiping God, "like from the Methodists, the Lutherans, and the Catholics." Sallie Lowry, the treasurer, said they should do some "fun things," so the group would not be just like school. Nobody mentioned the Easter sunrise service.

As the school year began, the young people held an ice cream social that was a great success. The Rosses had a good time themselves, but they particularly appreciated the fact that young people had done all the planning, collected the ingredients, made the ice cream, drawn the crowd, and done a fine job all round. They made a total of $112 on the ice cream social alone.

They also began some serious Bible study, and asked the Reverend Mr. Jennings to come for three weeks to get them started. He brought some commentaries, different versions of the Bible, and a concordance; and he did a good job of showing the young people how to look for answers to questions about the passages they did not understand. Susan's desire to study the Gospel of John got them going, and then they proceeded to the First Letter of Paul to the Corinthians.

The young people decided to plan for the spring a series of visits to other churches: Baptist, Methodist, Lutheran were in town. They would have to go to Arlington if they wanted to visit Roman Catholic or Jewish places of worship. Jim went to work on the arrangements.

A portion of their money, and lots of time went into planning for Thanksgiving baskets for needy people of Centerville. The young people, with active encouragement from the Rosses, took a total of thirty-five baskets to elderly people and those out of work. The whole church honored the youth by calling attention to their service to the community in a morning worship in late November. They even clapped—loud applause—when Mr.

Jennings told what they were doing. Well over half the baskets went to black families that the social welfare worker said were in desperate need. Jim, Tom Miller (whose family owned a large dairy farm near town), and Pete Lowry took the baskets around on Thanksgiving Eve. "It was beautiful," they said. "Everybody thanked us very much."

At Christmas time, the youth group sang carols at the homes of members of the congregation who were shut-ins. Then they all went to the Rosses for hot chocolate and doughnuts. They also sent money to some missionaries in Japan in the name of the whole congregation.

In February, Jim told the officers of the group that they would be welcome in Arlington at St. Williams Catholic Church and at B'rith Shalom Synagogue on succeeding Sunday afternoons in April. He said that visits of the local churches were set up too. He had noticed a Mt. Zion Baptist Church in the black neighborhood, and he wondered if that might not be fun to see too. But the other young people argued that they already were seeing one Baptist Church, and that they wanted some time to continue Bible study. So all decided that Jim had enough visits for them.

On March 24, only three weeks from Easter Sunday, Mr. Jennings called Gene. He said that he was very embarrassed; but at the local ministerial meeting someone had asked how plans for the Easter sunrise service were going, and it dawned on him that he had previously accepted responsibility for the service. Each year one youth group took charge, and he wondered if this would throw a monkey wrench in any of their plans. He apologized profusely for stepping out of line to speak for the young people, and he asked Gene to see what he could do about it. Gene assured him that the young people would help out, and he called an emergency meeting of the officers to figure plans for the event.

The young people said yes they had known about Easter sunrise responsibility being passed around the churches, but they did not think it was their turn. Anyhow, that was no problem. Sallie volunteered to lead a meditation on John 20. "It'll be short, but sweet." Susan would read the Scripture and lead the singing. Jim was asked to contact the churches for publicity. And then they talked some more about the upcoming visits and about the retreat now planned for June. After the meeting, Ina said she really thought Bill Jennings should have come to the youth himself with his goof. Gene should have refused to take responsibility, since they had operated all year on the basis of youth initiative and responsibility. Gene agreed with her, but professed relief that it was all taken care of so easily. "Weren't the kids great!"

Evelyn Johnson, the school's only black teacher, came to Ina's room after school a few days later. Ina had consciously tried to befriend her during the now-almost-two-years since both had started teaching at Centerville, and she assumed Eve just wanted to talk.

"It's about time!" Eve said, half laughing and half skeptical.

"For what?" answered Ina, picking up the double side of Eve's expression.

"White folks goin' to let us in." Eve mimicked Deep South patois.

"In what?"

"Don't you know? In the Easter sunrise service. Jim Tenney was by to see Reverend Anderson yesterday, inviting us to come in a couple of weeks. He didn't say much; didn't ask us to help plan or anything like that. Our minister called me, because he wasn't sure how to respond. I told him that if they just wanted color in the crowd, they could bring quilts. Mr. Anderson mentioned your name, said Jim said you are an advisor for the group. He asked me to see you, to find out if anybody is serious."

"Why, Eve, I don't know much about it," said Ina. "You know, we didn't go to the one last year. I would naturally assume your church was one of those accepting responsibility in turn. That's evidently how it's done, one youth group does it each year in turn. Isn't that right?"

"Well, Ina," Eve replied, "I really don't know much about the sunrise service either, because black people have never been invited. I understand from Mr. Anderson that there is a Holiness Church of poor whites that doesn't even get an invite."

"Goodness," Ina said. "I'll find out about it and let you know. That's just a sign of our ignorance. I'm sure it will work out."

"I thought you would be able to clear it up. If they really want to involve us, I think that would be fine. But if it's just another silly game, well those days are over."

Ina thought about calling Gene at the office. Then she countered herself with, "That's just what we decided not to do." She waited until that night and called Jim.

"Hi, Mrs. Ross," he said.

"Jim, Evelyn Johnson saw me today about your inviting the Mt. Zion Baptist Church to the Easter sunrise service. She said they might be interested if you are willing to involve them in planning, but that they resented being asked as a token gesture. She also told me you had not invited the black church before, that they never had been there."

"Hey, hold on a minute Mrs. Ross. I didn't mean to cause you trouble. Sure, I invited them, but I didn't think about hurting their feelings. I just saw the church that day we passed out baskets, and I said to myself, 'Hey there's another church I never noticed.' So I asked them, but we really should get them in on things if they feel left out. Oh, by the way, I also asked some people at the Holiness Church on Border Road. I guess they haven't been asked before either. Do you reckon we ought to get them into planning too?"

"Jim, I guess we had better have another meeting to decide. Can you call the others and come over tomorrow night?"

"Sure, Mrs. Ross."

That was the beginning of the calls. The next day Joe Black called Gene into his office through a secretary (which he had never done before). He expressed intense hope that Gene and Ina could dissuade the young people from their radical idea of undercutting the sunrise service. "It's been a beautiful thing, Gene, the high point of the year for many people here in Centerville. Now I don't know whose idea this was, but I know it wasn't from you. We've grown to admire and respect you and Ina. I'm sure you would not want to ruin this for everyone."

Gene told Joe Black the sequence of events as he remembered

them. "No," he concluded, "it wasn't our idea. And it wasn't done very well for blacks or whites. But after all, they're Christians and people. I've even heard you brag on how Sam and Willie Jones are among your best craftsmen. They go to Mt. Zion, don't they?"

"Look, Gene," Joe got a little red in the face, "I don't want to argue over the merits of the Negro race. I want this thing stopped quick. Either you stop it or I will. I gave over half the money for that church, and Mr. Anderson will do what I tell him. Now you better go and find out how to stop it quick, or I'll get him to."

The Rev. Mr. Jennings called that night, just as Gene got home from work. He asked to speak to Gene when Ina answered. "Gene, hi! This is Bill Jennings. I just called to clear up this thing about Mt. Zion taking over our Easter service. I've assured several people today that nothing like that was happening. What about it?"

"Well, Bill," said Gene, "I guess you know about the mistake in planning. The kids are taking responsibility for the service, like you complimented them for doing about the Thanksgiving baskets. I understand Jim invited Mt. Zion Baptist and the Holiness Church, and neither had been invited before."

"The heck with the Holiness Church. . . . I'm worried about the Negroes."

"That's funny, Bill. They were worried about us. They were really pretty angry that we just invited them to come, not to help plan the thing. I figured you had rotated it in the ministerial association, but I was wrong according to Evelyn Johnson."

"It's not funny at all, Gene. And you should know that Mr. Williams of the Holiness Church wouldn't even let us ask Mr. Anderson to join us. We've got to do something now to keep from ruining this service."

"Listen, Bill, how is it the Holiness Church never took part, yet their minister was in your group?"

"Well, Gene. He wasn't active at all. I guess they did come a long time ago, but then we moved the service out to Moon Lake. I guess it was too far for them. But that's very much beside the point."

"All I can tell you, Bill, is that the young people are coming over tonight for a meeting. I'll pass along your concern. Good-bye."

About fifteen minutes before the scheduled meeting, Sallie called that she couldn't come. Ina asked why, and she said something vague. Jim and Susan were there, though, on time. During the evening the phone rang several times, both sets of parents (Jim's and Susan's), Mrs. Lowry, and Mr. Renfroe called to urge the Rosses to withdraw the invitation to Mt. Zion. Jim was certain that the youth group should invite Mt. Zion Baptist and the Holiness Church youth to help in planning the service. Susan thought perhaps they had been too hasty in the invitation, but that they ought now stick by what had been done and make the best of it. She suggested that they pray about the alternatives, and then they would meet with the Rosses, inviting the Rev. Mr. Jennings and Bill Stovall, again the following night. Susan and Jim went to their homes.

Ina and Gene took out the coke glasses and their coffee cups after the young people left. Gene said, "How about one more cup?" When they sat down in the kitchen, things were really quiet for the first time all day. "You know this thing will probably cost my job, if we go through with it," he told Ina. Then he added, "Probably yours too."

"Yes," Ina said, "I really can't understand the hubbub. Mt. Zion is mad. Our people are mad. Goodness knows about the Holiness Church. But now we have to stick by Jim. For the first time in my life, I'm glad we don't have children. We're free of this town pretty much. We've got money in the bank. Most people can't do what we're doing without getting crucified."

"You're right, I know," said Gene. "But until now we ate this place up. Why not long ago a guy from Arlington Furniture approached me about doing sales for them, and I laughed at his proposal. Now I had better explore their offer."

"Before we go running off, Gene, let's see this thing through. I'm already looking forward to Easter sunrise."

Chapter 2
Dante Cavallo

prepared by Paul F. Wilczak

Chaplain Joseph Mruz was on call at University Hospital. It was an evening early in December, and Joe was looking forward to Christmas as a much-needed break from his clinical-pastoral program. He had just seen some patients in the intensive care unit and was walking down the corridor toward cardiac care. The voice of the telephone-page operator broke his reverie with a call for the chaplain. There was no other minister in the hospital that evening. Joe hurried to the nearest phone and called in. He was instructed to call Dr. Meister's extension. Just a hint of anxiety touched him as he anticipated, "I'll bet it's Mr. Cavallo." He dialed the number.

"Hello, Bob. Joe Mruz here. What's up?"

"It's our problem patient—Cavallo has tried to walk out on us again."

"Where's he now?"

"He's in the lounge and demands to see a chaplain. It's a good thing you're here tonight. Since you know him, I won't have to fill you in on the whole story."

"Is his wife with him?"

"I called her a few minutes ago. She said she'd be here in half an hour with her daughter and son-in-law."

"O.K., Bob. I'll be right over."

Joe slapped the phone into its cradle and began walking

quickly toward the wing of the hospital where Mr. Cavallo's room was located. His tenseness was slowly mounting. "Mr. Cavallo again," he thought. "What should I do to minister to this man now?"

University Hospital

University Hospital was located in a large industrial city on the campus of a well-known, highly respected university. It consisted of five clinics and the medical school, a complex which occupied an entire city block. A new wing was under construction as part of a long-range plan to expand physical facilities. Directly across the street from the medical school a multimillion-dollar life sciences building was rising rapidly. It would more than double the laboratory and research resources available to the hospital. The medical school, because of the prestige of its faculty and staff, which included several Nobel laureates, was considered outstanding. Admissions standards were very high and the work correspondingly demanding.

University Hospital had grown to its present size and preeminence during the last thirty years, and older patients sometimes remarked on the change. One woman, a secondary school teacher, had stated to Chaplain Mruz, "Things are different now. When I first was admitted here as a patient twenty-five years ago, my own family doctor cared for me then. He's dead now. Today there are so many doctors that treat me here. I don't know any of them well."

One of the best-attended courses in the medical school was a seminar on the dying patient led by Dr. Nikos Colicos, a staff psychiatrist. In the seminar, terminal patients were interviewed by Dr. Colicos and his assistants in a room separated from the seminar group by a one-way window. After the interviews the patient returned to his or her room, and the interviewers joined the seminar for a discussion. Dr. Colicos had completed the training program at the Psychoanalytic Institute in Chicago after his residency in psychiatry. While in Chicago he had been impressed by the work of Dr. Elisabeth Kübler-Ross in her seminar on death and dying. As a result he attempted to establish a similar seminar at University Hospital. One of the broader purposes of the seminar was to provide the medical staff with a forum in which to discuss their convictions on medical practice and hospital care. Members of the seminar included nurses, social workers, externs (medical students), clinical psychologists, interns, residents, faculty, and the chaplains in the clinical-pastoral education program (CPE). At one session Dr. Avery Baldwin, a hemotologist on the faculty of the medical school, expressed himself as follows: "It's nice to have a pleasant bedside manner, but what counts is medical skill. I would have no hesitation whatsoever in choosing the latter over the former. It's better to have both, of course, but a physician must first be a skilled professional."

In existence for over a year, the seminar had become a part of the hospital routine. Many staff members openly praised Dr. Colicos for his work and readily gave him their support. But things had been harder in the beginning, according to the psychiatrist. "Then it was very difficult to find support for my seminar. Many doctors were enraged at me for trying to interview their patients. Some of my junior colleagues even sought to humiliate me in public. A dying patient can be very threatening to a physician. Such a patient forces you to admit your own limitations. Perhaps more important yet, he forces you to face the possibility of your own death."

Dante Cavallo's Condition and Hospitalization

Mr. Dante Cavallo, forty-three, was admitted to University Hospital for the treatment of malignant lymphoma. He was married and had three children—Julie, eighteen, who was married to Adam Blank, twenty; Bill, twelve; and Charlie, ten. Mr. Cavallo had worked as a dance-band arranger before his illness. His home was located in a suburb about forty-five minutes from the hospital. The family was Italian-American, and all members were practicing Roman Catholics.

Mr. Cavallo had been in the hospital for about two months when Chaplain Mruz was first called to see him. At around 4 P.M. on November 22, the telephone page directed Mruz to call ward W-3. He was connected there with Dr. Robert Meister, a resident, who told him that a serious problem existed with the patient. Because Mr. Cavallo's malignancy had spread throughout his body affecting his kidneys and intestines most severely, their functions failed, and waste materials were building up in his system. A dialysis treatment (removal of wastes by mechanically passing a solution through the abdomen), therefore, was vitally necessary. The patient, however, had refused to allow the treatment. He had stated that he would prefer a violent death to the continuation of his present disability. His wife had been told of his refusal and was expected at the hospital in less than an hour. Donald Yu, an extern on the ward, explained the history of the patient to Chaplain Mruz; he included the facts that Mr. Cavallo had been a paratrooper and that he seemed to have some kind of phobia about having tubes coming out of his body.

Chaplain Mruz then spoke with Mr. Cavallo for the first time. During that conversation Mr. Cavallo appeared quite exhausted and expressed himself in a weak voice; his statements were punctuated by long pauses. Among them were the following: "It's too much, too much . . . I've had enough; I can't take any more . . . It [the dialysis] is painful; it is . . . My wife—she will tell you what I've suffered."

After spending some time with the patient, Chaplain Mruz spoke to Dr. Meister.

Joseph Mruz: I've spoken to Mr. Cavallo, Doctor. But he was very tired and couldn't maintain a normal speaking voice.

Dr. Meister: Perhaps he's reacting to a sedative we administered earlier.

Mruz: He doesn't seem to have the will to continue. I attempted to reach him but found it very difficult to assess his responses to what I was saying. I tried to emphasize the seriousness of his choice. But I'm not sure he fully realizes his position. If he does, however, I think that ethically he can maintain his refusal. In a sense he has the right to choose death.

Meister: (Nods ambiguously.)

Mruz: Mr. Cavallo is a Catholic.

Meister: Yes, a very good Catholic, from what I can tell.

Mruz: That may be an advantage now. I'm a Catholic seminarian, but I'm not ordained yet. If a priest would come to administer the last rites, this might create the mood necessary for him to become aware of the implications of his refusal. I want to consult his wife about this, but since she hasn't arrived yet, I'll call a local rectory and explain the situation. What do you think of this idea, Dr. Meister?

Meister: I think it's excellent, but I doubt if it'll change him.

Mruz: Well, there doesn't seem to be any alternative for us now.

Chaplain Mruz called the church. A priest was not available, but a message was left. Shortly afterward Mrs. Cavallo entered the ward; Donald Yu pointed her out to Joe Mruz. After Joe introduced himself, they both entered her husband's room. She became very emotional and began pleading with Mr. Cavallo. "Honey, don't give up now. You've gone through so much already. Don't let it go to waste. O, please, Honey! I need you! Don't leave us!"

Chaplain Mruz reinforced Mrs. Cavallo's plea by pointing out her love for her husband and by calling on the man to muster his strength as he had done in the past. Mr. Cavallo remained silent for a moment; then he haltingly began to speak: "I . . . I will . . . I will do it then. They can go ahead."

As Chaplain Mruz hurried to tell Dr. Meister of Mr. Cavallo's statement, Dr. David Epstein, the psychiatric resident on call, arrived at the nursing station. Dr. Epstein had been called by Dr. Meister because Mr. Cavallo had been heard to remark that he would prefer jumping out of the window to having those tubes stuck in him again. Upon notification by Chaplain Mruz, Dr. Meister and his team of assistants moved into Mr. Cavallo's room and began the dialysis procedure. During that time Chaplain Mruz and Dr. Epstein met and talked about what had just happened. Joe Mruz expressed his anxiety about the crisis, and the psychiatrist asked him whether he would like to sit in on his interview with Mr. Cavallo. Joe said he would very much. They agreed to meet with Mr. Cavallo shortly after Meister's team had completed their work.

During that interview Dr. Epstein carefully checked Mr. Cavallo's reality orientation and found it to be sound. He listened to Mr. Cavallo intently, occasionally interjecting a short remark or a question. At the close of the conversation he inquired as to whether a visit next morning would suit the patient. Cavallo agreed, and Epstein promised to stop by at ten. The chaplain again was invited to be present.

After the morning interview Dr. Epstein and Chaplain Mruz talked about Mr. Cavallo. Epstein said, "He's cogent but very depressed. When he said that no one at the hospital was his friend, you interjected, 'I want to be your friend.' To him that's bullshit. Don't *tell* him you want to be his friend, *act* like a friend. What he needs is someone he can count on. When you say you'll be by to see him, don't let him down. And don't let his silence get you down. Since he's so depressed, he's unlikely to feel like talking very much."

Two days after Thanksgiving, Mr. Cavallo dressed and tried to walk out of the hospital to take a taxi home. He was stopped by a nurse who recognized him, and Dr. Meister called on the Rev. Karl Koch, the CPE supervisor, for help. In the discussion that followed, a compromise was worked out with the patient, his family, and the doctors whereby Mr. Cavallo would be allowed to visit home in a few days. He would be permitted to leave in the morning, if he agreed to return to the hospital before evening.

Dr. Avery Baldwin, a noted hemotologist, had been consulted on the case. He called on Mr. Cavallo with a class of interns later on that day. Chaplain Mruz was visiting the patient at the time and heard the exchange.

Dr. Baldwin: How are you today, Mr. Cavallo? These doctors would like to have a look at you with me. Is that O.K. with you? Good. You seem to be looking better since your dialysis.

Cavallo: How am I doing, Doctor?

Baldwin: Well, you're not out of the woods yet. But we're doing what we can. Now, if you don't mind, I'd like these doctors to notice some things about your condition.

The Current Situation of Opinion on the Cavallo Case

Various staff members had stated their opinions to Chaplain Mruz on different aspects of Mr. Cavallo's situation.

There was Dr. Meister's position: "I would permit Mr. Cavallo to go home for a visit, if we could get his blood count where we want it. But the therapy isn't working the way we had hoped. And if it doesn't work soon, I imagine we'll be calling on you and the shrink again. We can't hold Cavallo here, if he insists on leaving. But if he does so against our advice, he'll lose his insurance coverage and won't be able to be readmitted."

Chaplain Mruz had consulted with Koch, his supervisor, on the effectiveness of his ministry to Mr. Cavallo. They discussed Joe's verbatim of his first visit with the man.

Joe Mruz: Mr. Cavallo seemed estranged from his manhood, from his wholeness. He needed support in his ability to act. I wanted to help him feel free to choose for himself in a very real sense.

Karl Koch: If this was your goal, then you did not act consistently to achieve it. You did not lift up his ambivalence so that he could make a choice. Why was that?

Mruz: Well, Dr. Meister had expressed a great deal of trust, and perhaps even hope, in me during his request for my aid. I tried to be completely honest with him in expressing my evaluation of the situation. But I also wanted to make it clear that I was there to help *him* as well as his patient. After the dialysis had been begun, Dr. Meister said to me, "Sometimes a little psychotherapy can work miracles."

Koch: It appears that you presented yourself as a deputy of the doctor while you dealt with the patient.

Mruz: It sure seems that way now. I was pretty scared too. Mrs. Cavallo's presence made me feel a lot better. She was very direct and affectionate in expressing her need for her husband. I was very pleased that the mood I had sought to create proved to be so very congruent with her feelings. In this way we were able to support each other. She also needed to feel she wasn't alone in this crisis. And without her appeal, my message would not have moved the man.

Koch: Be careful though, Joe. If Mr. Cavallo had been a stubborn man, your approach might have mobilized his resistance. As things turned out though, when Meister, Mrs. Cavallo, and you ganged up on him, the uneven odds carried the day. What kind of theology were you working out of?

Mruz: Well, I guess I wanted to give him the courage to be by calling to mind the danger he had surmounted in the past and the fact that he was still in a position to master his present disability. I tried to put this in the theological contest, I mean *context,* of a spirituality of suffering within communion, with loved ones.

Koch: OK, but don't overlook the possibility that *his* choice might not coincide with what *you* would have him choose. If *you* are in communion with him and love him in Christ, this implies your respect for his suffering and for his feelings in general. Try to be more aware of the feeling level of experience and communciation, Joe. I like your creativity and initiative, especially your decision to seek help and informal supervision from Dr. Epstein. Remember, however, that the feeling dimension is vitally important to ministry—*your* feelings as well as the feelings of others involved.

Mruz: Right now I feel more helpless than anything else. Sometimes Mr. Cavallo won't talk at all. Sitting there in dead silence can really drive me up the wall.

Koch: That is a very difficult but typical problem in hospital ministry. Let's bring it up, if you like, in our next group session with the other chaplains.

The next time Joe spoke to Dr. Epstein, the psychiatrist described Mr. Cavallo as psychologically rejecting his hospital environment in favor of one of his own choosing. As the doctor put it, "Mr. Cavallo simply wants to go home." He continued,

"Some doctors wouldn't agree with me—they see their duty as keeping the patient alive. But I believe that in such extreme illnesses with a clear prognosis of death, the patient should be allowed to die where he wants. I think he has a right to go home. I don't believe his death will be a painful agony. Renal failure usually means a gradually deepening coma and a quiet death."

Joe Mruz could appreciate more and more the positions of his two supervisors. A remark Dr. Colicos once made, however, kept coming to mind, "We should never give up hope when caring for the dying. Hope is one of the great medical intangibles. I myself have been surprised in the past by amazing remissions. This value, however, is very difficult to put into practice in an empathetic yet realistic way."

Joe often talked about Mr. Cavallo with Pierre Ponce, a third-year medical student from Canada, who had a great deal of familiarity with this patient. Pierre came from a family in which the practice of medicine was a tradition. Both his father and grandfather had practices in rural Ontario, and his younger brother was also in medical school. Pierre added another perspective: "I did extra work on Mr. Cavallo's case as a private night nurse. He was a very lonely man. I think he appreciated just the fact I was there on nights when he couldn't sleep. There were a lot of those nights. During the day things move fast at the hospital. No one has any free time. American hospitals are very high-pressure institutions. And some of the doctors, especially Meister, really can't relate to people, even if they have the time and want to. And Mr. Cavallo is an unusually tough challenge. It can cut into you to know there's nothing you can do for him medically."

Joe also had talked with Chaplain Peter King, a fellow student in the CPE program, soon after the first crisis with Mr. Cavallo. Peter was the chaplain assigned to Mr. Cavallo's floor. There was some question as to who should take responsibility for his pastoral care. Pete made it clear where he stood. "I just avoid seeing Mr. Cavallo. I don't know what to say to him. I'm a Unitarian; he's a Catholic. He's dying; I can't help him. I dread even going past his room. He looks like living death. You're a

Catholic. Maybe you'll have something to talk about, something more in common. Go ahead and take over."

Mr. and Mrs. Cavallo

Once when he talked to Mrs. Cavallo, Joe heard her say, "It's so hard to go on, so hard to see Dante like he is. The boys won't even come to visit their father. They can't take it." She spoke of the difficulty of daily travel to and from the hospital, of her feeling that her husband probably wouldn't recover.

Mrs. Cavallo: Dante was so afraid of death. He didn't even want to think of it, didn't want to buy life insurance for a long time. He thought such things would bring misfortune. But now his fears have come true.

Mruz: That's very hard to accept, I know. It's hard for all of you. Dante wants to go home though. Have you thought of the possibility of his spending his remaining days at home?

Mrs. Cavallo: I couldn't do it; it would be too much for me. We couldn't take it.

On December 3, Chaplain Mruz spoke to Mr. Cavallo. As of then he had still not been home for a visit. His physicians had not been satisfied with his blood count.

Mruz: How are you today, Dante?

Dante Cavallo: The same.

Mruz: How do you mean?

Cavallo: I can't eat; I can't sleep; I can't even move my bowels. Sometimes I just feel like throwing up.

Mruz: You've had a pretty hard day then.

Cavallo: I just don't want any more of this. I lie here alone so much. I know they'll want to stick those tubes in me again. I'm so uncomfortable.

Mruz: It sounds like you're a bit apprehensive.

Cavallo: I don't want those tubes anymore. I'd rather jump right out that window.

Mruz: Jumping out the window seems easier to take.

Cavallo: Yes, yes.

Mruz: Would you care to talk about that a little?

Cavallo: What's there to talk? I just don't want to live like this. This isn't living.

Mruz: It's very hard for you here at the hospital.

Cavallo: I just want to go home. I want to get out of here. I can't stand it. I feel alone. I just want to get out.

On December 5, Dante Cavallo made a second attempt to leave University Hospital. Again he was apprehended by members of the staff. Joe Mruz was on call and answered the page for a chaplain. While walking, Joe imagined another confrontation in the lounge similar to the one after Dante's first attempt. There would be Dante, his wife, his daughter, his son-in-law, Dr. Meister, and the rest of the staff on the case. Only this time Joe's supervisor would not be in the "hot seat"; Joe would. As he hurried down the corridor, Mruz almost wished it would stretch on without end, like a tunnel into eternity.

Chapter 3
The Death of Fanny Grimes
prepared by Louis Weeks

When Rick Noble had to go into the city anyhow, he determined to stop and see Fanny Grimes at the hospital. She had
been there off and on for the past two years. Rick wasn't
comfortable about visiting in the hospital, but he reckoned few
people from Lynn got into town who would go by to see her.
The Grimes lived on the outskirts of Lynn, and they also stayed
on the edge of the congregation. Fanny and George had always
been kind of independent folk; and while Rick had known
them over a long period of time, he did not see them often. The
Grimes had formerly owned a hardware store in Lynn, and
George still worked for Lonnie Beane who bought him out five
years ago. Since Fanny's illness, though, George worked only
on Wednesdays and Saturdays. He was almost fully retired,
probably sixty-five or so. Fanny must have been a couple of
years younger.

After he made the business calls, Rick Noble parked and
asked at the information desk for her room number—502.
Fanny looked pale, with machines and tubes, medicines and
charts around her. She still greeted him with the usual, "Rick
Noble! How's the family?"

Rick tried to focus attention on her face, pretending not to
notice all the things in the room. "Fine. Gladys wanted to come
with me, but I had some business to do. We're all fine. How are
you feeling?"

"Oh, all right. Little dull pain here and there. They take good care of me here though."

"Same kidney acting up?" asked Rick.

"I think it's worse than normal. They say some fluid gets around in my body and makes me feel worse than I have been. Did you see George outside?"

"No, I didn't," Rick said. "Is he staying in town?"

A nurse whisked in, apologized for the interruption, and asked Rick to step outside a few minutes. "Is he one of your sons?" she said to Fanny.

"No, he's a friend from Lynn, member of our church."

"I'll see you, Fanny. I'd better get on home." Rick said as he retreated toward the door.

"I wish you'd see George a minute if you can spare the time," she called as he backed out. "And thanks for taking the time to come by."

"I sure hope you feel better soon," Rick waved good-bye; "I will look and see if he's outside."

George was sitting in the waiting room. Rick greeted him. "George, hi. I had to be in town anyhow, and I've been wanting to see you."

George motioned Rick to a chair. "Things aren't going so well."

"Fanny doesn't look good, . . . all that equipment and the tubes don't help," Rick said.

"That's the dialysis machine. We have one at home. It's never been used. I bought it for $9500 just last month. It takes the fluid out of her body, and they said we needed one. Then this . . ." George's voice trailed off.

"What. It didn't work?"

"I don't know. Never got to see. I called the City Equipment Company, and they won't even buy it back. No, she just took a turn for the worse, and they said she better stay awhile here. Now Dr. Knowland says the fluid has gotten in her lungs, and she'll just have to stay here as long as she keeps breathing. He uses all kinds of fancy words, but it amounts to my decision. Do I take her home to die, or do I keep her here and let her just die slowly . . . maybe next week or maybe next month?" George lit one cigarette from another.

"If I take her home, it'll all be on me. It'll be quick and pretty sure to happen in a few days. If she stays here, the hospital will be taking care of her. She's got the pain, and it won't get any better in that department."

Rick offered George a cup of coffee. They found a little room next to the instant coffee dispenser.

"Fanny and I have been married almost thirty-five years—it'll be that on March twenty-first. These last years have really been hard ones. You know she's been pretty sick for almost three years. Every two weeks, then every week, I had to bring her in to see Dr. Knowland. That was when things were going good. At bad times she had to stay here . . ."

"The nurse mentioned a son. I didn't know you had children." Rick ventured, and he had known the Grimes a long time.

"Yes, Tom and Bill—two boys—but they've been gone a long time now. Tom and his family live in Utah, a long piece from here. Bill never married. He works for Uncle Sam. We haven't seen either one for years. Tom writes every so often, or his wife Hazel does. Bill just sends us something every Christmas. You know, we've been together—Fanny and me—every Christmas was special. We took our trips after that buying rush. Told everybody we were doing inventory. Went all the way to Gulf Coast one year. Now this . . . What should I do? Take her on home? Leave her here?"

"What do the doctors advise, George?" Rick stole a glance at his watch.

"They won't tell me. They say it's up to me. That machine at home won't help now, though. It's never even been used, and the company won't take it back! How do you like that? If I take her home, she'll die quick. If she stays here it won't change much, just take longer probably. I sure wish somebody would just come out and tell me one way or the other. What would you do if it were Gladys?"

"I don't know, George. I really don't."

"It wouldn't be so bad if there was some chance of her getting better. I don't know even if they've told her how bad it is. She acts like we will be going home soon, like the times before. Now it won't help though. Should I tell her?"

"George, you have been really close for a long time. You must know best what to do."

"It's a lot on my mind. I never had to make a choice like this before. Wish I had somebody to share it with. Doctors use fancy words, but I just know it amounts to my decision. What should I do?"

Chapter 4
The Abortion Study Committee
prepared by Donald E. Miller

The Followers of Christ is a Protestant denomination with approximately two hundred thousand members in the United States. The Followers have reached beyond the United States with service projects in Europe and the Far East and mission activities in India, China, Ecuador, Nigeria, and Indonesia during the past hundred years. Historically, the Followers have been largely a rural people. They were among the first to reach the rich farm lands of Pennsylvania, Ohio, Indiana, Michigan, Illinois, Iowa, Kansas, and California. Most of the members are still located in those states, although an increasing number are involved in urban occupations. The rural-traditional ethos is prevalent at most church gatherings, although the larger churches tend to be more urbane and status conscious.

The Followers originated in the early eighteenth century as a result of the religious enthusiasm that accompanied the rise of Pietism in Germany. Along with radical Pietism, Anabaptist and Reformed influences shaped the early history of the Followers. From their beginnings, they have professed a strict and radical adherence to the New Testament as "their only rule of faith and practice." With the Anabaptists, they accepted adult baptism as the mark of entry into the faith. They have also insisted upon a strict adherence to the teachings of the Sermon on the Mount, to turn the other cheek, and to love your enemy.

The beliefs just enumerated led to their being quickly expelled from Germany in the early eighteenth century. They immigrated to the United States, settling in Virginia and Pennsylvania. They were often persecuted during the Revolutionary War because their pacifist position was considered to be Tory. This is certainly one factor which led them to move to the frontier. During the Civil War many of the Followers were able to win exemption from the military service by paying a specified sum. In recent years, the Selective Service laws have allowed them exemption from military service.

In 1881, a major split occurred in the church in which those who insisted upon a strict exercise of church authority withdrew from the larger group for which the church's authority over congregations and individuals became advisory and not required. Those who did not follow the church's official teaching were not automatically excommunicated. For example, it is estimated that during World War II only one in ten young men of draft age actually followed the church's instruction to become a conscientious objector to military service. Curiously enough, even those who have military experience tend to support the church's peace position when they are delegated to Annual Conference, which is a representative body of highest authority in the church.

In recent years, there have been many tensions between those who would perpetuate the tradition of the church as they have known it over the years and those who would seek to adapt their faith to a changing world. Year after year, they press contemporary justice, women's liberation, union with other denominations, an end to the war in Indochina, and similar issues. Many congregations are very small, with less than one hundred members, and cannot support a full-time pastor. Some members are leaving the church because they believe it moves too slowly; others are leaving because they believe it does not stand for anything. These tensions are a serious threat to the denomination.

The Annual Conference

The polity of the Followers of Christ is midway between a congregational and presbyterian type. In congregational polity local congregations and individuals can finally decide whether they will heed district and brotherhood conferences. Very seldom in recent years has a person or a congregation been disfellowshiped. People are often heard to say that the decisions of Annual Conference, the highest denominational authority, are not binding.

On the other hand, church polity does have considerable authority, although largely informal. The Annual Conference is made up of representatives from each congregation allotted according to the numerical size of the congregation. Congregations usually discuss issues to be brought before Annual Conference, and conference decisions are therefore highly representative. If a congregation is not satisfied with a conference decision, it may bring the matter before conference a second or a third time. Issues are brought to the conference in the form of a *query*, i.e., a question is put to the conference. Queries must be accepted by a local congregation and passed to a district conference. If the district conference accepts the query, it will then be passed to the Annual Conference. The result is that Annual Conference decisions are usually highly representative of the total membership.

The district conferences and the Annual Conference also have the power to designate funds, attempt to raise money, assist congregations to secure pastors, and to arbitrate difficulties. In case of a legal dispute, the district conference has legal possession of property. The net result is that the authority of districts and brotherhood is informal, but nonetheless very real. At the same time congregations can easily disregard the districts and the brotherhood, if they do not need their assistance. A number of congregations are presently going their own way with very little regard for brotherhood polity.

The relationship which obtains between congregations, the districts, and Annual Conference might be diagrammed as follows:

Annual Conference
(representatives from congregations)

District Conference *A*   District Conference *B*
(representatives from   (representatives from
congregations)   congregations)

Congregation *A*   Congregation *B*   Congregation *C*
Congregation *D*

Annual Conference itself is administered by a central committee, which meets often enough to plan and carry out conference arrangements. The standing committee receives queries and regularizes procedures. Annual Conference appoints a general board for an ongoing administration of conference decisions. The general board in turn employs a general staff who work fulltime for the denomination. In addition, Annual Conference often appoints study committees to work out answers to queries that have come to it by way of the districts.

The administrative structure of the Annual Conference is as follows:

Annual Conference
Central Committee
Standing Committee
General Board
Committee A
Committee B
General Staff

The Abortion Committee

In 1970, two separate districts, one in the East and another in Ohio, passed to the Annual Conference queries about abortion (Exhibit 1). One query asked for a position statement on abortion, and the other asked for study and guidance on the question of abortion. The action of Annual Conference was to appoint a study committee composed of five persons elected by the conference, one person appointed by the general board and one person appointed by Follower Seminary. The seminary has no official position in the church structure, but members of the faculty are often asked to serve on study committees.

During the floor discussion at the conference, several statements were made about the importance of women's deciding this issue, since it involved them most directly. Consequently, the five members of the committee appointed by conference were all women. The general board appointed a psychiatrist, and the seminary appointed its professor of ethics. Let us consider some of the background experience that each of these persons brought to the committee.

Sandra Green is a registered nurse with a specialty in pediatrics. She comments that the pediatrics ward is full of the tragedy of life. "People expect me to say that the children's ward is a happy, joyful place. Just the reverse is true. The unwanted children are those who remain, and we experience the tragedy of their lives. It is a crime that such children were brought into the world in the first place. Every mother who wants an abortion ought to have the right to it." Sandra teaches embryology to student nurses.

Mary Patterson is a counselor at State College in Illinois. Many young women come to her for counseling about abortion. She feels their agony as she works with them. "I believe that all abortions are wrong. However, that does not help the young woman who has an accidental pregnancy and would rather risk her own death than deliver the child. Once a mistake has been made, it does no good to keep condemning the person who suffers its consequences. We must find ways of extending compassion without saying that abortion is all right."

Nelle Foreman is the wife of a college pastor. She and her husband have a constant open house for any young person who wants to come. They are a very popular couple, and their house is always a buzz of activity. "We always wanted children and were never able to have them. We have been able to adopt several children, but we had to wait for several years before a child was available. I just don't feel as competent to deal with this question as some of the rest of you. I think we have to understand the situation of a woman who faces this problem."

Tricia Mansfield is the wife of a pastor who just recently graduated from Follower Seminary. She is the youngest member of the committee and would bring her baby daughter along to committee meetings. Tricia actively campaigned to have the abortion law changed in the state of Washington. "Women have a right to decide what will happen to their own bodies. It is completely unfair that laws should dictate to women what they should do with their bodies. Nobody but a woman really understands what agony an unwanted pregnancy can bring to a mother. I know it is killing, but it may be necessary to kill the fetus in order to improve the quality of life. The quality of life is just as important as the fact of life. Think of the tons of pollution produced by every American baby during his lifetime in comparison to a baby anywhere else in the world. Abortion is necessary to improve the quality of life everywhere." Tricia was not a Follower before marriage.

Lartia Major is a graduate student in theology at a well-known midwestern university. She comes from a prominent Follower family in Pennsylvania and is strongly motivated to compete and achieve. She is married to a Roman Catholic student of religion whom she met at the university. "We must begin by admitting that abortion is a sin. It is the consequence of a sinful society. Not until all of us have confessed our sinfulness and our complicity do we have any right to say anything else. Not until we have put our lives on the line by offering time and money to help those in need, not until then do we have any right to criticize. We must prayerfully and penitently try to stand in the other person's shoes."

Daniel Ripley, M.D., is a psychiatrist who has been practicing for more than ten years. He is the director of the community therapy program of a mental health clinic sponsored by a religious denomination and located in the Midwest. Frequently women are referred to him for psychiatric determination of whether abortion is indicated. On several occasions, he did approve of abortions for girls who came to him. He feels now that other medical men may be sending cases to him when they themselves are unwilling to indicate abortion. "It is very important to allow a woman to think through the problem in a nonjudgmental atmosphere so that she can discover where her own inclinations and values really lie. The usual condemnatory attitudes of so many people merely complicate the problem for the person who is trying to make up her mind. It is also highly important for a woman to have support from caring persons around her so that she is not isolated at the time of her greatest need. Given this support, she will herself give more value to the human life growing within her."

David Masters is a graduate of an Ivy League school in the East with a doctor's degree in social ethics. He has been teaching at Follower Seminary since graduating from his doctoral program. He has been much interested in counseling and has been a frequent spokesman for the peace position of the Followers of Christ. He has no direct acquaintance with anyone who has sought an abortion. "The taking of human life is clearly wrong. However, the biological fact of life is what we mean by human life. We must try to understand the relationship between the human and the biological. If the fetus is fully human from conception, then we simply may not take its life for any reason short of threat of another life. It is important that we study the Scriptures as we try to characterize the emergence of human life and our attitude toward it."

The Work of the Committee

The committee met shortly after its appointment to identify its task and lay out its work. In keeping with the wish of Annual Conference that women have a strong voice in the committee, Lartia Major was appointed chairperson. During the initial meeting, there were strong disagreements about what the task was, how it was to be attacked, and what recommendations were to be made. After much debate, it was agreed that at least four areas of consideration were of importance, i.e., biblical, sociological, medical, and moral. The latter was to be in the form of guidelines for moral choice drawn from the other three areas. The first meeting ended with the agreement that David would work on the biblical area, Nelle and Tricia were to develop the sociological study, Sandra and Dan were to explore the medical concerns, and Mary and Lartia were to write the guidelines for moral choice.

The committee met a second time several months later to edit its work. There were strong contradictions between the sections that had been worked out independently. Long debates were able to resolve a few of the contradictions, but left others unresolved. Finally, the committee decided to ask Lartia and David to edit a report and submit it for publication prior to the 1971 Annual Conference. In spite of the infelicities, the committee wanted to know whether the Annual Conference would give any support to what they had done (Exhibit 2).

Hearings on important issues are always held prior to the consideration of that issue on the floor of conference. There was standing room only at the hearing with the room packed to capacity, perhaps a total of five hundred people. Debate was vigorous. The scriptural references were questioned. The suggestion that women who resort to abortion may not feel guilt was heavily questioned. Many considered the report confused, of no help, and incomprehensible.

During the actual business session, the floor debate was equally heated. One effort was made to dismiss the committee and drop the issue. That effort failed. Another motion would have enlarged the committee to include two more conservative voices had it been passed, but it too failed. The report was recommitted to the committee with the instruction that it give more consideration to the spiritual nature of sexuality and instruction in methods of birth control. Furthermore, the committee was instructed to see that the issue was discussed throughout the brotherhood.

Following Annual Conference the committee found that its chairperson, Lartia Major was leaving the country and all communication with her would have to be by mail. The committee quickly resolved to develop a study packet to fulfill the instruction of conference to see that the issue be widely discussed. Furthermore, it was agreed to publish a working document in the *Visitor*. The same subgroups were asked to revise their sections in light of conference criticism and to submit them to David for final editing. (The conclusion of the working document is given in Exhibit 3.) Each person was also to submit recommendations for a study packet. David was to develop a questionnaire and to make study packets available to those who wanted them. By this time scores of letters came pouring in to members of the committee. (See Exhibit 5, 6, 7, and 8. Exhibit 9 summarizes the work of a state-wide consultation service in the Midwest, of which a Follower pastor is state chairman.) Some condemned the church and the committee for even considering the question of abortion. Others praised the committee for its work. A few offered specific recommendations for changes in the report. Many articles pro and con appeared. One group called the followers fellowship developed a pamphlet called "Ways to Kill the Unborn." It deplored the liberal tendencies in the church and called the church back to the Bible. An article called "Abortion and War," which appeared in the *Visitor*, called Followers to adopt a stance toward abortion that is consistent with their attitude toward war (an excerpt is given in Exhibit 10).

Not many people requested the study packet, but hundreds filled out the questionnaire and returned it. (The questionnaire and the first 180 responses are summarized in Exhibit 4. The remaining responses followed very closely the percentages established in all categories of the first tabulation.) Some six hundred of the thirty thousand readers of the *Visitor* returned the questionnaire. Many responses were accompanied by letters with specific comments to each question. The range of opinion across the brotherhood was surely as great as that among members of the committee.

All this correspondence heightened the pressure on the members of the committee. Traditionally, issues of this type are not decided during the first year of discussion. It is, however, an unwritten law that they will be disposed of in some manner during the second year of discussion. The 1972 Annual Conference would certainly decide the matter one way or the other. The moderator of the conference, newly appointed year by year, became increasingly interested in the issue as conference approached. It would fall to him to moderate what could be a highly charged emotional session. Several pastors had already proposed to introduce a substitute paper of a more conservative character to replace the committee report. The committee was also under heavy attack by some women's liberationists because of the "sexist rhetoric" of its work.

EXHIBIT 1
I. Queries, 1970: Abortion

A. Whereas, abortion is a theological and ethical issue; and

Whereas, members of our churches are not clear what a Christian position on abortion might be; and

Whereas, some members have requested or may request guidance from the church on the morality of abortion; and

Whereas, several states have been revising abortion laws; and

Whereas, medical science has achieved great competence in performing abortions and detecting prenatal deformities and other abnormalities; and

Whereas, the 1964 Annual Conference statement on "Family Planning and Population Growth" does not give guidance for such circumstances as rape, mental health of the mother, and fetus abnormalities;

We, the District Board of the Followers of Christ, Ohio District, request the Annual Conference assembling June 23–28, 1970, to appoint a committee to draft and recommend to the Annual Conference a position statement on abortion. We suggest such committee include both sexes and professionals in theology, medicine, psychology, and civil law.

> Glen Cummins,
> Chairman of District Board
> Orpha Deeter, Clerk

B. Whereas, statutes regarding abortions are being changed by the legislatures and challenged in the courts in many of our states; and

Whereas, the question of abortion is essentially a moral issue relating to the nature of human life; and

Whereas, the Followers of Christ have never stated its position on the question of abortion;

We, the Mid-Atlantic District Board, taking into consideration the urgency of the issue, petition the Annual Conference to study and provide guidance on the question of abortion for the membership and congregations of the Followers of Christ.

David Rand, Chairman
of the Board
Raymond May, Secretary

EXHIBIT 2
Report of the Committee

Introduction

Because of the wording of the queries and the selection of the committee, we, the members of the committee, take it to be our task to offer a position statement for the Followers of Christ regarding abortion, which statement should take into account theological, social, medical, legal, and counseling considerations.

A Statement Regarding Abortion

Theological and Biblical Considerations

A Christian ethic regarding abortion should begin with the biblical teachings about life and about love, two of the central themes of the Scriptures. The Bible teaches us that life is a gift of God. This does not mean that man has no part in the beginning of life, for God has clearly given the cultivation and propagation of life into the hands of men (Gen. 1–2). Nevertheless, it remains a gift of God and is at center a mystery beyond definition, a mystery grounded in God's loving will and direction.

The Bible has little to say about the biological beginning of life, or about biological functions in general, except as they are a basis for moving, willing, acting. Blood is close to life, but blood in turn is a communion between persons, as in the Lord's supper. Body is important, not simply as a physical reality, but as a relationship between persons ("This is my body"). Breath is a mark of life in one account (Gen. 2), but breath in the Bible also refers to spirit and identity, as well as the giving and receiving relationships that constitute the living.

The beginning of human life is both a gift of God and a mystery of his creative power. It goes beyond the Scripture to suggest that conception is the beginning of personal human life, even though all the cells of the body are surely precious to God, and even though the fertilized egg must be doubly precious (the hairs of the head are numbered; no sparrow falls without God's knowledge). Biblically, however, human life is a personal interrelationship and not a unique assembly of chromosomes. Though precious in God's sight, the fertilized ovum is not clearly and unambiguously personal human life as the Bible speaks about it.

Abortion Study Committee

On the other hand, human life in the Bible is much deeper than viability, the time at which a fetus may be born and live. The heart is the center of life, and the blood is its presence. Movement and learning characterize life, both of which occur in very early fetal stages. The compassionate response of the community in preserving and nourishing the defenseless is a basis for life. Sensitive persons are moved with reverence in the presence of a growing fetus. If one cannot give a biblical basis for personal human life beginning precisely at the moment of conception, neither can one set some other point at which it begins. There is an indefinable mystery in the beginning so that we can say most appropriately of the developing fetus that personal human life within a supportive community is increasingly coming to be present. Long before the time of viability it is present in many ways.

This leads us to say that the termination of embryonic life in its earliest weeks is not clearly the taking of personal human life in the biblical sense. The command not to kill is based upon the value of personal human life as a gift of God. Just as the beginning of personal human life is a mystery that defies biological description, so also terminating early embryonic life is not clearly violating the commandment to refrain from killing. As the fetus emerges with more and more of the qualities by which the Bible describes human life, the terminating of that life comes closer to violating the commandment not to kill. This is not to imply in any way that early embryonic life is neutral or of no value. As we have already said, all the cells are precious in God's sight, and the unique cells of embryonic life must be doubly precious. Still, life in its beginning remains a mystery whose source is God, and we into whose hands has been given the possibility of propagating and terminating embryonic life, can act only in reverence for the God who, not only gives us life, but who has given his life for us that we might have the abundance of life, life eternal.

The Bible teaches that the fullness of life is love. The Creator of heaven and earth not only filled the earth with life and set man as a living interpersonal creature therein, but he entered into a covenant with man, promising to bring the fullness of life to him. In Jesus Christ we have the embodiment of love among men as well as the picture of what true life can come to be. The compassion we find in Christ certainly extends to every pregnant woman as well as to the developing life she carries. In Christ we are moved with compassion for those who have an unwanted pregnancy. In him we are brought to confess those attitudes that condemn and control other people. In him we are motivated to work for institutions and services which fulfill life and which therefore lead to the condition in which all children are wanted children. In Christ we realize that the well-being of unborn life can hardly be served by violating the feelings and choices of the person who nourishes it within her body.

Believing that matters of religion and morality are ultimately voluntarily decided before God, Followers have never leaned primarily upon legislation to enforce competing claims that make up any society. Legislation brings people to conform to the external standards of a wider social consensus. However, the heart and soul of morality is in the free choice of persons who love their fellowmen. Christ's example teaches us that we are not to compel others to be moral, even when they are the "enemy." Followers have been unwilling to rely upon military force, police force, capital punishment, or religious inquisition.

It follows that Followers do not usually try to preserve morality by supporting or tightening legislation. Followers seek, rather, to develop helping institutions and services for those who suffer, to introduce a note of compassion. Wherever possible, Followers work for the extension of voluntary choice within caring communities that make such choice possible. Law serves to introduce some dependability within the changing circumstances of society, and as such, it changes according to such circumstances as, for example, whether population pressures are high or low. So Followers ought to work for laws that serve the common good, but ought also to look beyond law to voluntarily chosen love and compassion which alone can infuse a new spirit among all people.

Our Broader Social Community

Life is an arena of conflicting values and competing rights. Even the potential for new life, which has been one of society's most esteemed values, is coming increasingly into conflict with the life and quality of life of those already living.

This conflict between the born and the unborn is obvious in cases where the life of the mother is at stake if her pregnancy continues. However, there are other conflicts which are less obvious but equally difficult and urgent for society to resolve. Our inability to cope with these conflicts is reflected in the upheaval over abortion that we are presently experiencing.

The prospect of overpopulation and pollution is one of the more dramatic factors causing the conception of new life to be experienced as a threat. There is a limit to how many people the earth can nourish and sustain. If population growth continues, humanity will run out of space. While speculation varies as to when this may happen, the fact remains that it will happen unless the birth rate decreases or the death rate increases. An even greater threat than the lack of space is the lack of other resources. Ecologists have made it clear that the earth can and will be used up if we continue our irresponsible consumption and pollution. The United States has a unique responsibility since its population expansion is a far greater threat to the earth than that of any other country. This is so, not because we are filling up space faster (we are only 6 percent of the world's population), but because we use a far greater portion than our share of the earth's resources (moderate estimates reaching as high as 45 percent).

Conception further threatens existing life and values as a result of the inability of the society to integrate the situations it has created into the value systems it has maintained. We have, for instance, all too many situations where the birth of an unwanted child is inevitable, but at the same time unbearable. When a society finds itself unable to provide acceptable alternatives, inevitably persons will be tragically caught in dilemmas which are literally forced upon them. The question for social policy is whether a society can be compassionate enough to foster attitudes and establish institutions that support and deepen life rather than control and destroy it.

Whereas a hard society has no personal concern for a young woman who cannot accept her pregnancy and resorts to methods which endanger or terminate her own life, a compassionate society seeks to preserve life by so valuing the life of the mother that she is not threatened by the life she bears.

Whereas a hard society tends to accept neither the child nor the woman who bears it, a compassionate society cares for the unwanted by providing adoptive homes, by accepting and supporting the mother who chooses to keep her baby, and by providing assistance in nurturing the qualities of that new life.

Whereas a hard society lacks sensitivity toward the woman who has already given birth to two defective children and is threatened by the possibility of a third, a compassionate society seeks to give love and support to her as she is confronted with her moral decision.

Whereas a hard society permits the already undernourished children to go to bed even hungrier, a compassionate society is sensitive to the suffering of all its members and is thus concerned that each one can be self-sufficiently productive in that society.

Whereas a hard society subjects the innocent to overpopulation, with attendant famine and death, a compassionate society promotes population control by means of family-planning and birth control.

Our reverence for God's creation and our desire for the abundance of life causes us to affirm all existing lives and all fetal life. Because we partake of God's universal community, we ourselves are torn when any men suffer spiritually or bodily. Our concern for others urges us to strive toward sharing our goods and voluntarily restraining family size because we believe the sacrifice of any life's abundance is in conflict with our responsibility.

Medical and Counseling Concerns

The biological sciences and medicine have raised more issues than they have provided answers related to abortion. Modern contraception has made pregnancy a relatively deliberate and free option. The risk to life and physical health of the mother with respect to pregnancy and delivery is now small; the physical risk attendant on clinical abortion procedures in the first trimester of pregnancy is much smaller. This risk increases, however, as pregnancy progresses. In contrast, the risk to health and life of the clandestine, unhygienic, often desperate, abortion procedure performed in our society at the present time is exceedingly high, and there are many deaths yearly. Further technological advances in the utilization of intrauterine devices (IUDs), the "morning-after" pill, and the seemingly imminent appearance of effective oral medication that will abort by chemical means, promise to make it increasingly difficult to delineate contraception from abortion. Existing public laws with respect to abortion, therefore, appear to become increasingly irrelevant and unenforceable.

Technology in the area of genetic and congenital abnormalities of human development have made possible increased knowledge about the detection of carrier states of defective genes and chromosomal defects and greater precision in the prediction of such disease in potential offspring. Some such conditions are diagnosable in mid-pregnancy, but not before. Genetic counseling considers the degree of risk involved, the seriousness of the possible defect, the parents' willingness to risk having a defective child in the hope of having a healthy one, the possibility that a defective child might be helped by medical or surgical procedures to achieve a more nearly normal life, the possible result of the defect on the life of the child, on other members of the family, and on society.

The ability to effect life and death creates paradoxes that are exceedingly complex. For example, the doctor may use heroic measures to preserve the life of a fetus of the same gestational age as one that could be legally aborted in some states. He may find he has struggled to save the life of an unborn child who is unwanted by the family. He may perform a sterilization procedure for a woman of the same age as another he is treating for infertility.

Human life has been seen by some simply in the potential of ovum or sperm, by others as beginning with fertilization (conception), and by yet others as the capacity for human interaction. Prior to interactive functioning, human life is not easily distinguished from animal life—yet, when can we say interaction begins? At quickening? At birth? Or prior to conception when parents wish for a child, and their feelings and behavior are altered by their fantasied interaction with it? Further, the discrimination between mere existence and a distinctly human quality in life is universal. Neither in terms of any one point in time or development nor in any other measurable quality can science provide the definition to this discrimination. It seems most meaningful to view life as a continuum or developmental process.

Psychological studies of women who undergo the abortion experience have not supported generally held beliefs regarding the emotional stress of such an experience. In the majority of cases there is general relief and no guilt reaction. In some, a brief and mild reaction occurs, and more severe disturbances occur rarely. Among psychiatrically disturbed women who undergo abortion there is generally no loss of stability and, sometimes, even improvement. Frequently expressed beliefs regarding the occurrence of involuntary infertility, difficulty in sexual functioning, as well as depression, are not supported by the available evidence.

Psychological studies of children and of family life have brought a new and increasing concern by behavioral scientists for the problem of the "unwanted child." There is a broad consensus that the status in early childhood of being unwanted is devastating with respect to personality development and the occurrence of behavioral and emotional problems.

Regarding all these paradoxical, complex, and sometimes conflicting values, the counselor is called upon to relate to the person first of all. He is asked to care and to care enough that he would not want to control or dominate or use another for his own purposes, but rather to set him free to grow and to seek out his own highest purposes. This requires a highly personalized view of every issue and every moral choice. Secondly, but not less important, the counselor and physician must also function in a context that can reflect and preserve the freedom of moral choice of the other and be consonant with his values and highest purposes.

With those who struggle personally with these issues, the larger community and sometimes the church has tended to deal distantly, impersonally, and judgmentally. If no longer expressed in legal prohibition, these attitudes tend to be preserved through isolating responsibility in the hands of the medical profession. Professional people, as well as their patients, have need for persons of the faith community who will undertake to share the burden of moral decision and thereby bring a fuller humanity into the lives of all.

Guidelines for Moral Choice
As Followers in a troubled world, we seek proper guidelines to make moral choices.

—We believe that life from its earliest beginning is valuable.
—The context in which we make moral decisions is that of God's compassionate love of all men in Jesus Christ.
—We can never be happy to negate life, be it by abortion or other expressions of withdrawing love and support from fellowmen.
—Compassion is a more Christlike approach to troubled human situations than tight control.
—Responsible decision in Christian community calls one to think of all concerned, not only of one's self or situation.
—We believe morality is a commitment in freedom of men in interpersonal relation before God.
—We can best reach out to affirm the life of the unborn child by compassionate response to, rather than condemnation of, the mother; by assisting her to cope with her situation, we help her achieve greater capacity to give of herself and accept this budding life.
—Because God creates and values all his creatures, we ought not love those whose values are most like ours more than those whose values are not.
—We believe abortion is the expression of a deeper problem—of the failure of men to be supportive, loving community.

Believing that in Jesus Christ we are brothers with believers and nonbelievers, we speak to our social community and with other Followers regarding the matter of abortion and the value of human life.

191

To our common human community, we urge that citizens take into account moral freedom, interpersonal and communal sensibilities, and medical and social knowledge as the legal boundaries marking the limits of permissible interaction are defined.

—Because in the first trimester of pregnancy there is medically less risk to the mother, because socially the wider community (including medical attendants) has less investment in the life that is to be born, and because theologically the concern for terminating pregnancy increases as the fetus becomes a fuller participant in our common world, we urge that the termination of pregnancy, only during the first trimester, be at the request of the community, family, or individuals concerned, governed, of course, by the laws regulating medical practice and licensure.
—After the first trimester, we consider abortion of far more serious medical, social, and theological import as it more deeply involves the total human community, and suggest that only when evidence that the woman's physical or mental health is endangered or that the fetus has serious physical or mental defects ought abortion be legalized.

We confess our faith that Christ spoke truly, that whatsoever we do to our fellowmen, we do to him.
We incarnate our commitment to God
in our relationship to our fellowmen.
We receive bountifully, but we misuse the bounty of life:
We withhold love and forgiveness from those whose acts we reject.
We condemn those who would abort an unborn life and then condemn parent and child to social rejection, hunger, living death.
We seek to overlook our little faith and selfish love by pointing out and asking punishment for our brothers' wrong.
We pray for forgiveness and commit ourselves anew:
As children of God, we commit ourselves to affirm life at its inception;
The lives of Followers with whom we share common values;
The lives of Followers who choose values opposing ours.
As brothers of Jesus Christ, we commit ourselves to support life toward its fullness:
By reexamining our needs and abundance and the simple life;
By caring for unwanted children, chronic welfare families, jobless, hungry, imprisoned, ill.
As fellowmen with all who inhabit God's earth, we commit ourselves to moral responsibility.
Because God gives and sustains life in interpersonal community, we pledge ourselves to protect and support all life—unborn, joyous, suffering —entrusted into our universal human community.

EXHIBIT 3
Annual Conference Working Paper

A Position Statement

Followers strongly believe that all human life is sacred and that personal life is the fullest expression of human life. The question of abortion should therefore be discussed within the context of renewed sensitivity to the wonder of the personal human life and of human sexuality. We believe that abortion should be considered an option only when all other possible alternatives lead to greater destruction of personal human life and spirit. We rejoice with those who voluntarily give birth at great personal sacrifice. Yet we also support those who after prayer and consultation find abortion to be the least undesirable alternative available to them and those they love. We believe that such persons should be able to make their decisions openly, honestly, and without the burden and suffering imposed by an uncompromising community. Furthermore, we advocate that all who seek abortion should be granted sympathetic counsel about various alternatives as well as the health and safety of publicly available physicians and hospital care.

Some Implications

It is vital to the church that it educate its members about the sacred spiritual quality of human life and human sexuality, so that the question of abortion may be considered in proper context. The church should provide study packets, current reading, study groups, church school classes, workshops, and personal acquaintance with the experience of those involved in abortion decisions. Much further education regarding sexual relations, family-planning, the meaning and practice of responsible parenthood, and the value of persons is crucial to the spiritual and social well-being of the brotherhood. This effort should be both an individual and collective responsibility. The brotherhood should support other organizations such as Planned Parenthood and Clergy Consultation Service in their educational efforts.

Responsible parents should seriously consider limiting family size, since overpopulation poses a very real threat to the whole of human life. However, contraception and voluntary preventative measures, such as vasectomy, are always preferable to abortion as a form of birth control.

The brotherhood should do everything it can to make it possible for a mother to want and care for all her children. We can best show our concern and compassion by providing homes for women who do not want the unborn child and for children who are unwanted. We need to foster a fellowship of families and counselors who would welcome and care for such women and their children.

In some situations abortion is perhaps the least undesirable alternative available. Decisions in such situations are most nearly genuine when made with consideration for all persons involved. Such situations include serious threat to the lives and emotional well-being of the mother and her family. The precise definition of circumstances must be left to the mother, the father, the physician, the pastor, and other significant persons in whom the mother has confidence. (Situations such as rape, incest, and malformation of the fetus need not necessarily lead to abortion, if they do not seriously threaten the emotional well-being of the mother and the family.)   Any person who considers an abortion should receive the best counsel about options available, including adoption and foster care. Such counsel should encourage her and those close to her to work through the decision, keeping in view the value of human life, the consequences of the various options available, and the well-being of those most directly affected. We oppose any action, direct or indirect, by parents, physicians, the state, or anyone else that would compel a woman to seek an abortion against her will. When abortion is performed, it should always be done under acceptable medical care, and as early in the pregnancy as possible.

Physicians are urged not only to consult with their medical colleagues, but also to seek other ways to share the burden of moral responsibility so frequently thrust upon them. They are encouraged to resist the inclination to shoulder the weight of decision in isolation from others who are involved and concerned. The meeting of minds, whenever possible, of caring persons most involved and most to be affected by decisions that are made, gives dignity, moral sensitivity, emotional support, and personal security to all concerned. Any physician or attendant who, because of personal moral conviction, chooses not to perform or participate in an abortion, however legal, should be free to do so in good conscience, amd should receive the full support of the church. We urge a physician with such convictions to refer patients who may desire an abortion to another competent certified doctor.

Followers may in good faith work for changes in laws regulating abortion practice. Many existing laws add to the guilt and degradation of life. We support those who conscientiously act for the repeal or alteration of such laws.

EXHIBIT 4
Discussion/Survey Checklist on Abortion

The following checklist may serve either as a guide for personal study, a starter for group discussion, or a form for responding to the Study Committee on Abortion. In looking ahead to final revisions of the report the committee earnestly welcomes the reactions and comments of *Visitor* readers.

1. Abortion is a question appropriate for the church to consider: ( ) Yes ( ) No
2. Human life should be considered fully personal at the time of (check one): ( ) conception ( ) quickening: when motion is first felt ( ) viability: capable of surviving after birth ( ) birth ( ) some other time

Abortion Study Committee

3. The following is sufficient reason for abortion (check any number):
( ) threat to the mother's life
( ) threat to the physical health of the mother
( ) rape
( ) incest
( ) fetal deformity
( ) possibility of fetal deformity, e.g., rubella
( ) threat to the well-being of the family
( ) threat to the mother's emotional health
( ) threat of overpopulation
( ) the desire not to have a child
( ) other:
4. Civil law should continue heavily to restrict the practice of abortion, as it now does in most states: ( ) Yes ( ) No
5. A woman has the sole right to decide what happens to a growing fetus within her body: ( ) Yes ( ) No
6. Every woman who seeks an abortion has the right to full medical care: ( ) Yes ( ) No
7. The church should provide more teaching, counseling, and other services regarding attitudes toward sex, family planning, and abortion than it now does: ( ) Yes ( ) No

Tabulation of Responses to Discussion/Survey Checklist on Abortion

1. Abortion is a question appropriate for the church to consider:
   Yes   147
   No   29
   No answer   2
2. Human life should be considered fully personal at the time of (check one):
   conception   72
   quickening   15
   viability   31
   birth   29
   some other time 19
      (1—As the development of relationships begins)
   no answer   7
   don't know   4
3. The following is sufficient reason for abortion (check any number):
   threat to mother's life   148
   threat to the physical health of mother   117
   rape   123
   incest   111

fetal deformity	116
possibility of fetal deformity, e.g. rubella	104
threat to the well-being of the family	79
threat to the mother's emotional health	89
threat to overpopulation	43
the desire not to have a child	57
other: (1 each)	8

    1—mother's age—too young or too old)
    2—any reasons given by mother
    3—anything else a parent feels sufficiently harmful to child
    4—tubular pregnancy
    5—self-control taught in the home and church

no answer	13
none	8

4. Civil law should continue heavily to restrict the practice of abortion, as it now does in most states:

Yes	72
No	101
No answer	5

5. A woman has the sole right to decide what happens to a growing fetus within her body (emendations: 1—if unmarried; 2—"a woman *and her mate* have"; 3—if married, husband should be consulted, but woman should have final decision):

Yes	71
No	98
No answer	10

6. Every woman who seeks an abortion has the right to full medical care:

Yes	133
No	22
No answer	16

7. The church should provide more teaching, counseling, and other services regarding attitudes toward sex, family planning, and abortion than it does now:

Yes	157
(1—"abortion" deleted)	
No	17
No answer	4

EXHIBIT 5

To the Study Committee on Abortion:

Let me respond to your questionnaire published in the Visitor. *We have been studying the abortion issue in our church for several weeks now, and I want to express my opinion to you.*

1) *Certainly it is a question that ought to concern the church, for it is both a personal and a social issue.*

2) *I agree with the conference statement that the fertilized ovum is sacred from the time of conception, but that the fetus is not fully personal until the time of birth, when the newborn baby can begin to enter into relationships with others.*

3) *I cannot say when the reasons listed become strong enough to indicate an abortion. It depends so much upon the circumstances.*

4) *Many of the current laws in many states are very destructive. They could be liberalized without affecting the population trends.*

5) *The mother does have a right to decide, but she ought always to discuss the matter with her husband, doctor, family, and other concerned persons.*

6) *Medical services should be available to all persons. No one should be denied contraceptive or abortion services just because she is poor.*

Sincerely,
(signed) Jacob Smith

EXHIBIT 6

To the Annual Conference Study Committee on Abortion:

I am sick of all the talk about abortion. This is something that ought not even be discussed in the church. Can't the church discuss spiritual things rather than getting mixed up in things that don't even concern it.

Everyone knows that abortion is murder. It is against God's law, and only those who do not read their Bibles favor abortion. It is just as wrong to kill an unborn child as to kill one that is ten years old. If you want to kill a child, why don't you pick on one you are living with. You don't have to fly to another state to do that.

Nobody worried about overpopulation before this. God has taken care of us so far, and he will continue to do so. If your mother had had an abortion, you wouldn't even be here to talk about it. You should be concerned about your soul rather than overpopulation.

There is so much immorality today. Laws permitting abortion will just allow more immorality. We need to return to God and live by his laws again.

Sincerely yours,
(signed) Agnes Hunt

EXHIBIT 7

To the Annual Conference Abortion Committee:

Your statement is just full of words that mean nothing. You write on and on, but what have you said when you are finished. If you would only write with the simplicity of the gospel, we would know what you are saying.

Why is it that we take pages to get ourselves confused? Why can we not come right out and say, "All abortion is wrong?" We have stated in a conference paper, "All war is sin." Why can we not be so clear and direct about abortion?

It is not all the qualifications that help us know what to do. We want to know directly what is right and what is wrong. Each person is able to interpret that in his own situation. You can't do that for him in any event. Why don't you speak the truth to us in a simple, direct way?

Sincerely,
(signed) Alvin Hardy

EXHIBIT 8

Alvarez, Idaho

Dear Committee Members:

We of the Alvarez Church have given the abortion issue serious consideration, and we want to come out strongly opposed to legalized abortion. We believe that the unborn infant is sacred and that terminating the life of the unborn infant is contrary to God's will.

We want our church to take a strong stand on this issue. We hope our ministers and teachers will teach the sacredness and holiness of life, and that our church will be known as one that stands against abortion.

(signed by twenty-six persons)

EXHIBIT 9

Statistics from the State
Pregnancy Counseling Service

State pregnancy counseling service is administered by a pastor who is a member of the Followers. He has been very active in organizing and expediting this service for women who have problem pregnancies. Some of the members of his own congregation have been critical of his efforts in this regard.

The counseling service has a hot-line number to which anyone can call for help. An interview is arranged, and the person is then helped to find the appropriate professional who can be of further help.

During the past two years, three thousand women have been interviewed, ranging in age from ten to forty-eight. Twenty-five hundred of these women have obtained an abortion. The further statistical description is as follows (taken from a sample of nine hundred women):

Interviewed:
  900 Total
  780 Chose abortion
    10 Decided to have the baby and be a parent
     8 Decided to have the baby and place it for adoption
    20 Married couples who decided to have the child

Women's status
  620 Single
  180 Married
   10 Widowed
   90 Divorced
  400 Students
  120 Housewives with no other employment
  120 Pofessional women
  280 Nonprofessional women
   30 Had previous induced abortion
  700 Used no contraception
   30 Hardship cases

Race
  860 White
   30 Negro
   10 Other

Religion
  640 Protestant
  140 Catholic
    4 Jewish
   20 Other
   96 None reported

EXHIBIT 10

To the Abortion Study Committee:

I was disappointed to see the abortion statement resorting to the argument for "the lesser evil." This is a ruse that has been so often employed to justify military action, and thus far the Followers have rejected that argument entirely. The proponents of "the lesser evil" will say that indeed it is true that all war is sin, and that the horrors of war are a curse. Then they go on to say that there come times in our national life when war is certainly preferable to any other alternative.

To this argument the Followers have consistently said that refraining from military warfare is not only a New Testament ideal; it is a life and a commitment to which we are definitely and specifically called as Christians. Turning the other cheek is not only a nice saying for children; it is God's actual possibility to those who believe in him. The gracious possibility of God in Christ is our way of life.

When the abortion study committee speaks of the "least destructive alternative," it is surely resorting to the "lesser evil" argument. Do we not believe that God's gracious way of life is available here also? Indeed there will be situations which will bring much agony to a pregnant mother, and indeed we always look for a pleasant alternative. Does God not offer another possibility to those who believe in him? Is abortion not an evidence of hardness of heart? Surely, from the beginning it was not so. Are not all children to be wanted, and has not anyone who ever considers abortion already sinned? Let us then speak of God's gracious possibility rather than the lesser evil.

Sincerely,
(signed) Dan Bales

Part IV.
Methodology of Cases
Chapter 1
Transferring Professional Training Models: The Case Method— for Theological Education?

prepared by Fred K. Foulkes

During the 1971–72 and 1972–73 academic years it was my privilege to serve as senior adviser to the Case-Study Institute, a small organization whose chief assets seemed to be vision, imagination, and a strong determination to try something different. The something different was to be an attempt to apply the case-study method, as practiced at the Harvard Business School, to theological education. I was to be the consultant on methodology, and what happened during those two years was exciting, and has, I believe, great implications for the future. This brief article will discuss the rationale for the case method at Harvard Business School, suggest possible parallels to theological education, cite some evidence in support of those parallels, and speculate some about what is needed in the future.

To start, I would like to say something about the case method as we have developed it and used it at the Harvard Business School.

Case Method at Harvard Business School

The principal mission of Harvard Business School is to train men and women who are two to three years out of college to become future general managers, people who will allocate resources in an efficient and effective manner, who will act in a socially responsible way, and who will manage corporations like communities. Thus, men and women are being trained to be action-takers and decision-makers. These general managers will think critically of the long-run as well as the short-run, and they will know how to define and resolve problems, sifting through data and examining alternative courses of action in light of company goals and objectives. And they will know how to implement action plans, getting results through the actions of other people. Needless to say, they will also know how to read blueprints and balance sheets, the difference between fixed costs and variable costs, and they will know that they have to continue to read and to learn. Rather than training students to become good students of business, we are training them to become good business people.

With such goals, it becomes clear, I believe, why the case method is a teaching tool that makes much sense for us. Cases describe real problems, and, through the study and discussion of hundreds of cases while a resident here, the student gets to practice in a low-risk environment the critical skills that he will need as a general manager. Students, daily, are forced to wrestle with actual business problems; they must figure out which facts are significant and which ones are missing; and they must try to apply concepts and techniques and to build solid analyses based on the facts found in the case. Moreover, they must be prepared to defend their solutions in front of equally well-prepared colleagues, who are in possession of the same facts and who have mastered the same concepts, tools, and techniques.

The methodology, then, is consistent with the task, for when the student, many years later, is in the shoes of the general manager, specific tools and techniques will be forgotten or outmoded, but the process of defining problems, thinking conceptually, being able to put things into a framework and see the larger picture, and developing action solutions will, presumably, be the same. In addition, the method carries with it a motivational kicker. Because professors don't lecture and because cases are discussed by students in class, the student has to assume responsibility for his own learning. (With the case method, when one is unprepared, little benefit is derived from the class discussion.) When one participates, one has a vested interest in the discussion and its outcome; and students, when the case method is operating well, are involved, motivated, and committed.

It should be added that the professor's role in case-method teaching is a unique one. He, too, is a participant in the discussion, and he, too, wants to feel that he has learned something, whether it be a new insight, a different framework, approach, or point of view, or perhaps a solution to the case which he hadn't thought of and never had heard proposed before. While the professor provides some input and some direction and structure, depending upon his own teaching style and the nature of the subject matter, it must be emphasized that he, too, is a participant in the discussion and this resource-facilitator role is, at least at first, not an easy one to which to become accustomed. As part of his job, he may push the students, not only to be logical in their analyses, but also to be specific in their action plans. He also may summarize at the end of class, giving his own views of the case. And while challenging students and encouraging students to challenge one another, he, too, needs to be prepared to be challenged by the students. Needless to say, he must be well prepared in the sense of knowing the case and the conceptual material, and, in addition, he has to demand excellence while at the same time establishing a climate in the classroom that is conducive to learning.

But for Theological Education?

To the extent that the theological student is preparing himself for the ministry, he, too, needs work in the seminary which will prepare him well for his future role. He, too, needs to be able to define problems, to choose among alternatives, and to implement action plans. He, too, needs to be able to see situations for all their richness and complexity and to understand how to get results through other people, and, all the time, provide spiritual leadership. Well-prepared and well-taught cases drawn from the life of the church would appear to be a useful part of such a training process. My two years of experience with the Case-Study Institute convince me that this is indeed the case, and I am excited about the prospects.

Related to my work with the Case-Study Institute, I have also had the opportunity to teach in three continuing education programs for ministers. In preparation for these workshops, ministers were asked to state the areas of their ministry in which they felt the most need for improvement. Interestingly enough, the areas of understanding the nature of the gospel and understanding the purpose of the church were rarely mentioned. Most frequently mentioned were the following: theological understanding for the ministry; practical leadership in parish administration; techniques for group leadership; communicating with people through preaching, teaching, and conversations; and applying the gospel in the modern world. The case method is a tool well designed to meet these needs, and it was our experience that the case method was extremely effective in these continuing education programs.

The participants in these programs were also asked to answer in writing the following quite revealing questions: "As you look at your ministry, what are your irritations and frustrations, your satisfactions." Their responses proved interesting indeed; and some of the comments listed under irritations and frustrations included:

Spiritual apathy and inertia—lack of "community" among church members.

Inability of groups to realize their respective responsibilities and to work together to accomplish their goals (and my own seeming inability to help them in this realization).

Lack of understanding on the part of individuals of the minister's task.

Lack of enthusiasm about church and its ministry . . . "petty" problems to be cared for.

ADMINISTRATION, especially details. When I end up doing things myself because it's easier that way, and then find myself caught with too many things to do to have them come out well.

Failure to communicate how to put the gospel to work practically in our lives—in relation to how we treat each other personally and in larger issues of politics, war, welfare, ecology, etc. . . . Lack of real leadership ability among lay people for teaching, chairing committees, etc. . . . Unwillingness of lay people to make use of training opportunities already offered . . . Ambiguity in my role in relation to the organizational structure . . . Not enough time to get it all done . . . Poor follow-through . . . Sermon preparation slow.

That I am considered no businessman and am therefore thought unable to administer the program of the church—that this is the function of the board, and I should stick to "religion" which means visitation, preaching, and hospital calling.

Getting people involved at a depth-level in worship, study, and witness.

I get irritated by the pettiness of people. I get frustrated at the gap between peoples' capabilities and their activities, and at having to serve as "daddy" to some people of the parish.

The scarcity of leadership people who can and will take the church seriously, wrestle with its reasons for being, plan and carry out comprehensive programs.

Organization for time-use in a satisfying manner; approaching and solving problems; leading parishioners into decision-making in a satisfying way.

Rigid church members who refuse even to discuss needed changes in the church. Church members who say that they want change and yet are not willing to do the hard labor it requires . . . Motivating people to explore the deeper dimensions of the faith.

The administrative aspects of the ministry . . . the lack of commitment on the part of many churchmen . . . the slow pace of change.

Too many "Mickey Mouse" jobs that are left to the pastor. Difficulty in recruiting laymen for vital lay ministry. The difficulty church members have in arriving at an adequate understanding of the purpose of the church.

Inability of lay leaders to do solid planning and to follow through on responsibilities. Conversely my limitations in transmitting on to them what I do know about these processes.

Lack of cooperation among area clergy. Lingering lack of discipline in my use of time. Fighting the same battles over again (mission of the church, etc.).

If one were to classify these comments, they fall, it seems to me, under three broad headings: spiritual apathy, leadership and/or administration, and the communication of the gospel and the understanding of the church. It is interesting to note, however, that the leadership and/or administrative problems predominate, and this is consistent with several conversations I have had with members of the clergy. Many ministers have told me that in seminary they learned much they do not find useful, and much of what they need to know to perform effectively is either not taught or not emphasized enough; and while these comments say something, not only about the need for continuing education and about the work in the seminary these men and women had in preparation for their profession, but also about the use of the case method in theological education. This is because cases could, by exposing students to the kinds of problems they will face, help prepare them to deal with similar situations after they have graduated. The comments also serve as a guide to what kinds of cases should be developed and taught in the seminary classroom and in continuing education programs.

The limited experimental use of cases with seminary students and with parishioners has also been quite positive. Students take to the method quickly and become very involved in class discussions. In a similar vein, parishioners identify with the problems in the cases, and after a few discussions seem ready to move from the problems at someone else's church (the case) to problems of their own church (the real case).

Whether whole curricula or entire courses or simply parts of courses become case-oriented is an open question, but one that eventually needs to be addressed. To begin to answer it the churches and the seminaries must decide what a minister needs to know. Once there is some consensus around that question, the issue becomes how best to teach it. However this comes out (and it will and should have differing results for various institutions), it is my bet that case studies will play an important role, chiefly because of their potential for learning, but for student motivation reasons as well.

If entire courses become case-method oriented, it is important to recognize, if the Business School experience is relevant, that the cases would be supplemented by notes, readings, and conceptual pieces. For the idea is to move inductively from readings and cases to generalizations. And from studying and discussing a series of well-written and well-chosen case studies, a set of generalizations (or at least a set of important questions) will emerge. For instance, if the question of church purpose is an important one, it is my guess that producing and studying a set of cases concerned with large, small, and medium-sized churches of different denominations struggling with the question of purpose would result in some meaningful generalizations and questions, ones which would be important to present and future ministers and to church people generally. At a more mundane level, the study of a number of case studies about the use of church property would tell us much, I believe, not only about the uses of church property, but about the nature of the church and ministry.

If this is to happen, many cases will have to be written, and because cases go out of date so rapidly, it will have to be a continuing activity. In addition to training in case-writing, training in case-teaching and course-development is essential. The work of the Case-Study Institute is a beginning, a good beginning in my judgment, and it needs to be continued and further supported and strengthened.

This book is also a beginning, and I hope it is useful in testing out the model and in refining it for use in the seminary classroom. The case study has the potential to make theological education more professionally oriented and less graduate-oriented. It has the potential to motivate students and to give them simulated experiences of what the "real world" will be like. While it is not as good as field work and experience, case study is a viable and useful substitute and supplement. And as Henry Ford is reported to have once said about the school of experience, "It is the best teacher. The only problem is that its graduates are too old to go to work." It is my guess that in time cases will find their way into the so-called soft fields as well as the "hard" disciplines. I believe they will be used in the practical fields as well as in the theoretical disciplines. I would even suggest that they may serve to blur the distinction between fields and that this probably would be a good thing. I also think they will foster interdisciplinary work, and this will be both challenging and threatening.

I hope that students, professors, and parishioners will experiment with the cases in this book, for a model with such potential deserves to be tried. After some experience is gained, this pilot project can be evaluated and decisions about its future can be made. But it needs to be first tried out, and in that venture I wish you well. I hope that from study and discussion of these cases our measure of theological awareness will be increased and our lives enriched.

Chapter 6
Writing and Teaching Cases
prepared by Ann D. Myers and Louis Weeks

I say that the strongest principle of growth lies in human choice.
George Eliot, *Daniel Deronda*

Writing Cases

A typical case study presents students with a problem situation and asks them to choose a solution and outline a plan of action to implement their choice. The case studies in this book are modeled after those developed at the Harvard Graduate School of Business Administration. Like those, they are based on data obtained from actual situations by means of field research. Typically these cases have no single "right" answer, although some solutions are acknowledged to be better than others. All of them offer a dilemma, a knotty problem, for consideration. For example, in the "Greg Wright and Twin Rivers Presbytery" case a minister is caught between the conservative attitudes expressed by some members of his denomination and the insistent demands of his own conscience; a priest in the "Dante Cavallo" case is anxious to preserve life yet unwilling to prolong suffering; a group of laity at "Walnut Avenue Church" is divided over how to make the best use of funds available to the church. All these situations will provoke radically differing responses and suggestions for action from students.

A case study usually asks that a decision be made on the basis of the facts in the case and that a rationale be constructed for ways in which this decision may be put into effect. A case may raise questions at many levels. It may seek for plans to solve a

problem of resource allocation or a plan to raise the consciousness of certain people involved in the situation. It may be the
locus for ethical reflection. A case may be used in an evaluative
way, to raise the question of what the selection of a particular
set of goals says about our values and the ways in which we
choose to order our lives. It may also raise theological questions
of commitment and doctrine, meaning and alienation, life and
death. In order to sustain analysis on all these levels the writers
have sought to present in these studies a richness of factual
material while at the same time endeavoring to construct the
cases in a streamlined form so that they will be manageable
during a class session.

Some cases seem, at first reading, to present just a slice of life.
However, as any student of literature knows, each *tranche de vie*
has its own peculiar slant. Case-writing and case-teaching are
closely interrelated, and the particular slant of a case is determined in part by the use to which it is to be put in the classroom. Thus, before we go further in our discussion of case
teaching it is worthwhile to pursue the subject of case selection
and case writing.

Case Selection

While a number of cases are presently being made available
through the Intercollegiate Case Clearing House at Harvard
Business School, it is likely that you will select one or more
situations and begin to develop your own cases. In this event,
some of the pointers which follow may be of use to you.

Material which gives the promise of yielding a good case
study is called a case "lead." It is important to be discriminat-
ing when choosing a case lead. A situation may look promising
to an outsider, but when the lead is pursued further the re-
searcher may discover that either there are no substantial conflicts or else they are too poorly articulated to bear investigation. It is helpful to bear in mind four simple criteria in your
selective process:

1) Does the situation pose some kind of dilemma, a problem for
which there is no easy solution?

2) Are the participants in the actual event willing to cooperate with you and enable you to gather the information needed?

3) Is there a person or organization who is willing to take responsibility for "releasing" the case? Case studies are assumed to be confidential until written permission or "release" is given for them to be used in a specific course, educational progam or textbook.

4) Does the study of the situation relate to a course need or objective?

Case leads can be found in newspapers, magazine articles, denominational reports, through conversations with friends, or through personal experience. Harvard Business School issues a caveat to its researchers against the latter involvement because the writer as participant can fail to achieve sufficient distance from the real case to write the document objectively. On the other hand, if you can assemble enough data whether by interview or through "inside knowledge" to recreate the situation, and if you can subject the case to the critical eye of another person for helpful distancing, then an "insider" case may prove valuable indeed.

Perhaps a brief word of warning may help you avoid one of the common pitfalls new case-writers encounter. You may be tempted to piece together a case from generalized experience, but you would do well to abandon this idea. The case that emerges full-blown and credible from the mind of the case-writer is truly rare. One can scarcely manage the internal consistency in such a case, and often an air of unreality pervades it. By the same token, if students know the case material to be based on a real life event and not just a series of impressions which have been manipulated to produce a certain outcome, then they are more likely to give it serious consideration.

Case Research

It is best to try to be introduced to the participants in your case situation by someone with whom they are familiar. The best church cases are often constructed from data which is found in controversial and emotion-laden arenas of human interaction. It is difficult for people involved in such situations to open themselves up to an outsider. Sometimes a proposal to write a case will meet with refusal. However, if the case is public enough, written documents may supply sufficient information.

It is important for you to be an accurate, if not meticulous, observer and recorder of facts. Events, opinions, chronology, biographical data are all important in establishing the network of circumstance which makes up the plot of the case. Asking yourself the following questions can help:

1) Are you obtaining sufficient information so the case will relate essential facts?

2) Have you given careful attention to the timing so that you know which event preceded others?

3) Do you have personal interviews with key people who represent the existing range of opinion on the issues? Are you representing the conflicting views with equal amounts of evidence?

4) Have you kept an open mind? If you can resist prejudicial and dogmatic judgments, you might discover an even richer case than you had hoped to find.

5) Are the persons involved in the actual case assured of confidentiality and agreeable to your using the disguise mechanism, if one is called for. In church cases, changing the name of the denomination, the name of the local congregation and the names of the principal figures in the case seems to provide a satisfactory disguise.

Writing the Case

Because putting together a case involves a unique approach with its own rules and conventions, writing the case is, for many people, the most difficult part of the process. A precise definition of case style evades articulation; roughly speaking it might be described as a hybrid composed of journalistic, artistic and literary approaches.

As a case-writer, you will need to adhere to some of the guidelines of good journalism. Unbiased reporting of the facts, with a high degree of accuracy is one goal to keep in mind. Cases, unlike articles, theses, and the like, avoid statements of opinion or hypothesis. The temptation to editorialize with statements like, "It was a typical board meeting" or "Mr. Johnson exercised brilliant leadership" should be resisted. If such perspectives on the situation are necessary, it is best to let the participants in the case provide them. Thus, the case might include such statements as: "Members of the board reported that their meeting was a typical one," or, "Mr. Johnson was acknowledged by the congregation to have provided them with brilliant leadership." In general, the case-writer states things which are to be taken as unalterable fact, while statements of opinion are reserved for the persons or groups who hold them.

To a limited degree, the case exhibits some of the characteristics of an art form. The case-writer, like the artist, operates within the restrictions of the form he has chosen. The following case form, or outline, is most commonly used and may be of help to you:

1) Introduction. A statement of the problem and a hint at various alternatives which the protagonist(s) are considering. Placing a concrete setting at the beginning of a case is a vehicle case-writers often use to get the reader immediately involved in the action-orientation of the case.

2) Exposition. Several paragraphs of background material serve to give the readers essential facts about the past and lead them to the present.

3) Development section. The central issues unfold in this part of the case. Included in this section are conversations among participants, reflections they make, and other significant contemporary data.

4) Summary or recapitulation of the problem.

5) Exhibits. Any pertinent material that would detract from the text by introducing an element of artificiality can be included in the case study "answer" to appendixes.

One of the keys to structuring a good case is a thorough preliminary analysis of the various issues in the case before beginning to write. Needless to say, it is important to focus these issues so that they relate to course or class objectives. Good case-writing is expressive writing. The case-writer does an analysis and then remains in the wings, letting both the facts and the characters' actions and opinions dramatize the story. One important job for you, then, is to learn how to symbolize or suggest a frame of mind, an approach to a problem, an attitude. A certain fact or statement may be used to represent a much larger reality. To a sharp eye a church budget can be a clue to the priorities and limits a congregation has assigned to the life of the congregation.

Several case conventions can help you maintain the illusion of reality that you are working so hard to create. Throwing the reader directly into the situation at the beginning of the case establishes the fact that the action is to be seen through the eyes of the participants. As a general rule the case-writer, a potential disrupter of the "willing suspension of disbelief" that a case creates, does not appear as a character.

By skillfully handling transition, you can allow the story to emerge in a natural way. The use of juxtaposition as a tool to enhance meaning and create drama is important to keep in mind. Other devices, such as recording small sequences of conversation verbatim, describing the environment colorfully, all add to the "reality" of the case.

A good case will operate at many levels of abstraction. While at one point in the discussion a student might be prevailed upon to discuss the pastoral versus the priestly responsibilities of a minister to a congregation, another time the students are pushed to decide what they would actually do to balance the two roles in the context of the case situation. In other words, a strong case is one which allows the instructor to ask both the abstract and the concrete question in the classroom. Part of the excitement of writing a case is knowing that you as its author are able to construct it with that built-in versatility. It is knowing that in many different ways the document you create has the potential to challenge students to make a choice; to challenge them to exercise their moral and ethical judgment. Perhaps this process will help them come to an expanded realization of what alternatives they are truly allowing themselves, and the extent of their opportunities for growth.

Thus far we have focused on a standard case format—a kind of "case orthodoxy." There exist a number of valuable alternatives in selecting and writing cases—a variety of potentially helpful "heresies" if you will. Case construction and collection is still in an experimental phase within theological education. As you experiment in case-writing and teaching, it is important that you share your insights and the new forms you discover.

Teaching the Case

The case study teacher is not the traditional dispenser of knowledge found in most classrooms; rather, he or she is a learner along with the students. The case teacher attempts to foster meaningful dialogue among students in as many ways as are possible but avoids structuring the outcome of the discussion in any way. If the case is germane to the objectives of the course, then the discussion it provokes will very likely be fruitful.

Those reading the case and preparing it will be focusing on a singular, albeit compressed, experience. This confluence of events may be unique and unrepeatable, but readers cannot help applying their own analogous memories and hopes, insights and attitudes, as they study it. By the same token, there can be no foolproof prediction of the resolution of the "knot" or problem. The struggle to meet the case with an ethical, theologically viable, coherent, and practical solution or evaluation is what the class time is about.

Those discussing the case probably share a number of common ideals and/or principles; they have no doubt undertaken personal quests for such intangibles as honesty, love, justice, peace. How the students rank these common ideals as priorities in the process of formulating solutions to case problems will vary immensely. Thus a specific "game plan" for each case would be next to useless. Because classroom, groups, and purposes are so divergent, only general suggestions will be offered.

The teacher must first probe the students' insight into the case. What *is* the situation, not just what does it *appear* to be? What changes are possible? Who can bring them about? How? What is the role of . . . ? How do formalized strategies fare in meeting the needs of this situation? Which responses cover more of the "pain" points? Why? Questions like these are useful in getting the discussion started.

Probe in as many ways as you can. When a student moves the discussion into areas you did not intend to focus on, keep with the person's insights so long as the group seems to be benefitting. When a person makes outlandish assessments or decisions, call on another student for evaluation. "What do you think of that, Susan?" "Does that sound fishy to you?" When imprecise words are used by students, try to restate them with sharper expressions if you can. Turn student questions back to the asker. "That's a good question. What lies behind it in the way of intimations about a solution?" In every way seek to explore the situation as an observer, analyst, and as an ethical person.

Your second job is to referee. As opinions and information surface, you will be tempted to press for consensus and to minimize conflicts and differences. But the temptation is well worth resisting. In the rarefied atmosphere of a classroom, you can even multiply the friction by exaggerating differences of opinion in order to stimulate critical reflection. "Bill, that's exactly the opposite of what Susan is saying." "Susan, what are you going to say to *that?*" "Why, that's not at all where Evelyn seems to be." "Harry, you're frowning. Does that sound foolish to you?"

Your third job is to oversee what is being constructed by the students. It might be that the group relieves you of this responsibility, but you have it until someone assumes it. Students may proceed to construct a model of the situation, rules for action, strategies based on the input from collateral readings —there are any number of options. They will not be able to solve all the problems or answer all the questions raised in the case. They may, however, address at least some of them. The best fun occurs when a group sets parameters and applies experience in depth to one aspect of the case. Whatever their process for addressing the situation, people can learn to trust one another as they discuss case studies, to learn from one another's contributions, to build on one another's suggestions. Practically speaking, the rudiments of social organization in general and of the church in particular are present in the very event of studying the case. People will exhibit cooperation, internal controls, leadership, mutual assistance, creativity—perhaps even courage. You are superintending these developments as well as the more obvious ones.

Here are some practical aids which other-case teachers suggest you might draw upon during class sessions:

1) *Role play.* You may wish to assign parts either to individuals or to the group as a whole, either for brief and informal periods or for more extensive times. "You are the session of the church, the advisors, the power elite, the blacks of the community."

2) *Votes.* "How many of you think they should just give up? Raise your hands. How many think they should organize? How many think they can fight it out by themselves? Commit suicide? Admit they are wrong?" etc. Calling for positions on less significant issues will often facilitate honest confrontation of the more important ones.

3) *Chair placement.* Do two or more students agree? Place them together in the room and let them "evangelize" others in their point of view. At some point you may have several groups seated around representing different opinions, changing their seats as they change their minds. It will increase side-conversations to do this, but informal learning may increase proportionally. You can always dissolve the groups of students if you encounter too much interference with the train of the discussion.

4) *Time limits.* It frequently helps to be aware of the time in dealing with cases, just as it does when one is involved in simulation games and counseling sessions. A warning of specific time limits on individual remarks will allow you the unquestioned right to interrupt the "sermonizer" who likes the

sound of his/her own voice. Students familiar with the case study process develop a capacity for putting a check on their overtalkative colleagues, thus relieving the instructor of this task.

5) *Honesty.* Admitting your own feelings will help others do the same. But it is not just with feelings that honesty is desirable. If the strategy sounds unbelievable or has been disproven in practice, you should say that you think so. "Blue sky," cynical, or other inappropriate language should be labeled as such. Remember the class has a right to rebuttal when you enter the fray.

6) *Call for evidence.* You don't want to foster legalism, to be sure. However, occasionally you need to refocus on the actual experience to be addressed. "What evidence have you that it would work?" offers an open possibility for response either from the case or from personal experience.

7) *Call on participants.* Frequently the pensive person can use a nudge. If the threat level seems low for almost everyone, it becomes easy to ask: "George, you surely have been quiet. How does that sound to you?"

8) *Observe the "little things."* Eye contact, noise level, body attitudes, and side remarks will help you know when to pause and when to move on if you are attentive to them.

9) *Relate contributions.* You can buttress the constructive process by rephrasing one person's words in the vocabulary of another. "Susan, is that what you meant by ———?" Teaching a case can be compared in some sense to playing a hand of cards. It is your job as instructor to remember what cards have been played and what important points have been left out. You are then in a position to relate contributions, build on points that have been made previously, and elicit responses in areas that have not been explored. In order to do this well you must have a thorough knowledge of the issues in the case and all the possible paths of action that might be taken, so that when a student makes a point its implication is immediately clear to you and you can (a) exercise judgment as to whether to encour-

age the student to push forward with the analysis and discover another related point, or (b) see that the student's statement conflicts with, or is an important part of, the assumption another student made ten minutes before. Some conservative professors at Harvard Business School say it takes a minimum of eight hours to prepare a new case.

10) *Closure*. It really is inappropriate to interject one of your cherished observations at the end of the session. If it is an important one it should be included earlier in the class. However, it is most appropriate to comment truthfully on the enterprise as people have experienced it. You can call on others for help here, too.

These admonitions on writing and teaching cases have been presented in a rather hortative way for you. However, we hope they will serve you temporarily as you gain mastery of this method of teaching and writing. Good wishes to you.

Resources on Case Study

Useful books on Case Study are:

Andrews, Kenneth R., ed. *The Case Method of Teaching Human Relations.* Cambridge, Mass.: Harvard University Press, 1960.
McNair, Malcolm, ed. *The Case Method at the Harvard Business School.* New York: McGraw-Hill Book Co., 1954.
Pigors, Paul, and Pigors, Faith. *Case Method in Human Relations: The Incident Process.* New York: McGraw-Hill Book Co., 1961.
Stenzel, Anne K., and Feeney, Helen M. *Learning by the Case Method.* New York: The Seabury, Press 1970.

Below are some of the articles on case study, bibliographies of case materials, actual cases, and teaching notes available from:

Intercollegiate Case Clearing House
Soldiers Field Post Office
Boston, Massachusetts 02163

Intercollegiate Bibliography, current volume, for annotated list of business administration cases.
Annotated Bibliographies of the Case-Study Institute
Business and the Urban Environment: A Guide to Cases and Other Teaching Materials.
"The Case Method" (mimeographed) a list of articles on the case study method.

CASE-BOOK

ON CHURCH AND SOCIETY

*Edited by Keith R. Bridston, Fred K. Foulkes,
Ann D. Myers, and Louis Weeks*

The Case-Study Institute was originated in affiliation with Harvard University to apply the case method to theological education. Each case study in this book includes: an actual event with background description, identification of the issues involved, alternatives for solving these issues, and an examination of the ethical and theological aspects. Some of the current controversial issues included are: internal church conflicts and changing attitudes on such issues as race, sex, abortion, war, and church government.

Useful for classroom discussion or as a means of learning or teaching by laity or clergy, Casebook on Church and Society provides new insights into many current social and religious conflict situations.

KEITH R. BRIDSTON is director of the Case-Study Institute of Cambridge, Massachusetts, and is also on the faculty of Pacific Lutheran Seminary in Berkeley. Fred K. Foulkes is assistant professor of business administration of Harvard Business School. Ann D. Myers has been assistant director of the Case-Study Institute. Louis Weeks is assistant professor of church history at Louisville Presbyterian Seminary.

ISBN 0-687-04709-9   An Abingdon Original Paperback